# FLORE NIGHTINGALE'S LONDON

AN

**A** TO **Z**

OF THE

**L A D Y**

WITH THE

**L A M P**

DEBBIE PEARSON

AND

JULIE CHANDLER

First published in the UK in 2021 by Pearson Chandler
Email: info@pearsonchandler.com   Website: www.pearsonchandler.com

Kind permission for the use of logo has been granted by the Florence Nightingale Museum. A CIP catalogue record for this book is available from the British Library.

ISBN: 978-1-7399550-0-7

Book design and layout by Dominic Xavier, London, UK.
Printed by Blinky Media, London, UK.

Typeset in Adobe Caslon 11/15pt and 9/12.5pt, with headings in Neuzeit Grotesk and LTC Bodoni 175.

# CONTENTS

# INTRODUCTION

2020 was the bicentenary year of the birth of Florence Nightingale. As part of the commemoration the Florence Nightingale Museum commissioned some guided walks around *Florence Nightingale's London*. The authors of this book, Debbie and Julie, were the guides who were leading these walks. Because of the pandemic these unfortunately had to stop. But, inspired by the Florence Nightingale Museum's online exhibition *Nightingale in 200 Objects, People & Places*, the idea of writing this book was born instead.

Using this book you can discover places in London with a connection to Florence Nightingale – these include addresses where she stayed; locations she visited; places her family, friends and colleagues lived and worked; where she did her shopping; and other sites connected to her life and legacy. It also gives you an opportunity to learn more about her story through places that still exist in London.

We have spent a lot of time in the company of Florence Nightingale while carrying out our research, and feel we have got to know her very well. We believe we are now on first name terms, so hope you will forgive us for referring to her as Florence in this book.

Florence lived a long life, and more than half of it was spent in London. We have included an overview of her life, to put her time in London into an overall context.

The main section of the book is an A to Z of locations. This includes addresses, postcodes and, where applicable, the names of organisations. We have been surprised and delighted at the variety of different places which have connections with Florence, and the wide spread of locations in the London area.

Some of the locations are clustered in particular areas, such as Mayfair, Westminster and the City of London. So, if you would like to go on a self-guided walk, we have included some suggestions.

We are indebted to the Florence Nightingale Museum for their support with this book, and have included a chapter to provide some more details about this wonderful museum.

Although the main focus of this book is London, you may wish to consider day trips or short breaks to other parts of the country, so we have also included some suggestions for you.

Florence was most famous as the "Lady with the Lamp" during the Crimean War. We have included a chapter explaining about this war, giving information on dates, locations and people. We have provided details about the recruitment of the nurses, especially the first 38 to arrive, the medical care and Florence's work. We have also highlighted the media interest, travel to and from Scutari Military Hospital, and what happened when the war was over.

The legacy of Florence Nightingale is still evident to this day. We have provided some examples of this, in London, in the United Kingdom and around the world.

Florence was very well connected and she interacted with a large number of people. We have included an INDEX OF PEOPLE, cross referenced to locations in the A TO Z section.

The COVID-19 global pandemic meant that the 2020 bicentenary celebrations were scaled back. Florence was a great champion of fresh air and hygiene – never more relevant than during a pandemic. We hope that this book will form part of the legacy of the bicentenary, and encourage people to get out and about in London in the fresh air.

We hope you enjoy visiting locations connected with Florence Nightingale. If you find any other places you think we would be interested in, please let us know. Our contact details are in the ABOUT THE AUTHORS section at the end of the book.

# THE
# LIFE
## OF
# FLORENCE
# NIGHTINGALE

## Florence in her youth

Florence was born on 12 May 1820 at the Villa la Colombaia, in the Italian city of Florence – where her parents were on an extended honeymoon. Florence's sister, Frances Parthenope, born in 1819, and known as Parthenope, was named for a former Greek settlement, now part of Naples.

Florence's father had been born William Edward Shore, but took the name Nightingale to receive an inheritance from his great uncle Peter Nightingale. Florence's mother, Frances (Fanny), was one of the 10 children of the Member of Parliament (MP), William Smith and his wife, Frances. The Nightingale family was wealthy and owned two properties: Lea Hurst, Derbyshire, where they spent the summer, and Embley Park, Hampshire, where they spent most of the year. They frequently visited London, staying in hotels or rented accommodation. Florence had many aunts, uncles and cousins, and often stayed with them.

Florence was educated at home – initially by a governess, but later, unusually, by her father. She learnt music, drawing, mathematics, sciences, as well as several languages.

At the age of 16, at Embley Park, Florence believed she had received a calling from God. She did not yet know what form her service to God would take. Her faith remained important to her all her life.

A young woman of Florence's status was expected to make a good marriage, have children and run her husband's household. Florence received a number of marriage proposals, but declined them all. The one she came closest to marrying was Richard Monckton Milnes, a poet and MP. He courted Florence for seven years, and although she turned him down, they remained friends.

*Drawing of Florence by her cousin Hilary Bonham Carter*

In her twenties, Florence travelled extensively with family friends, Charles and Selina Bracebridge. In Rome she met Sidney and Elizabeth Herbert, who became great friends. On the same trip, she also met Henry Manning, who became the Roman Catholic Archbishop of Westminster. They corresponded over many years, while she was exploring her Christian faith.

Florence and the Bracebridges spent 10 months, in 1849/50, visiting Egypt and Greece. When she was in Greece, Florence rescued an owl, later called "Athena", who became her pet.

## Florence's interest in nursing

As a child, Florence had helped care for people living in local villages. As an adult, Florence became interested in nursing, but her family was horrified. At that time, the reputation of nurses was poor – little better than housemaids, with dubious morals and frequently drunk.

She tried to persuade her family to let her train as a nurse, but they refused. She sought the opinion of the American physician Samuel Gridley Howe, when he and his wife visited Embley. He encouraged her, with "I say to you, go forward if you have a vocation for this way of life... you will find that there is never anything unbecoming or unladylike in doing your duty for the good of others."

Meanwhile, Florence had met the Prussian Ambassador, Christian von Bunsen, in London in 1842. He told her about the German Hospital in Dalston, and the work of Theodor Fliedner in Kaiserswerth, Germany. Through the ambassador, she arranged to travel to Kaiserswerth. In 1850 she visited the hospital and wrote about it; then in 1851, she asked to train with the Protestant Deaconesses. Her family reluctantly agreed.

*Kaiserswerth Deaconess Institute, 1929*

With the help of Henry Manning, she visited the Sisters of Charity in Dublin; and in Paris received training from the French Sisters of Charity. She also visited hospitals, including Lariboisière.

In 1853 she was appointed Superintendent of the Establishment for Gentlewomen during Illness, in Harley Street. There was no salary, but her father granted her an allowance of £500 per year. During 1854 there was a cholera outbreak in London, and Florence temporarily left Harley Street, to assist at the Middlesex Hospital.

*Florence in 1856*

## The Crimean War

After Great Britain joined the Crimean War in 1854, Florence was asked by Sidney Herbert, Secretary at War, to take a group of women to nurse the British soldiers fighting "in the East". It was this that made her a household name, and where she gained her nickname "the lady with the lamp".

Please see the chapter FLORENCE AND THE CRIMEAN WAR.

## After the Crimean War

In 1856 Florence was invited to Balmoral, Scotland, to meet Queen Victoria. Florence discussed with the queen the setting up of a Royal Commission, to learn the lessons of the Crimean War.

Florence moved into the Burlington Hotel, in Cork Street, London, nicknamed the "Little War Office" and started work on reforms aimed at improving the health of the British army. She worked with a number of close associates, including Sidney Herbert, statistician William Farr and John Sutherland, physician and sanitation expert.

She analysed data on sickness and mortality in the Crimean War, and developed a way of showing some of the important information as a diagram, which she called a "coxcomb", also known as a polar area diagram. In 1858, Florence became the first female fellow of the Statistical Society of London.

Having seen "pavilion wards" in French hospitals, Florence proposed reforms to hospital design. The pavilion style hospitals had long central corridors, from which led wards with high ceilings and large windows. The advantages included light, fresh air and good ventilation. These ideas were later published in *Notes on Hospitals*.

She also published *Notes on Nursing: What it is, and what it is not*, intended for use by those caring for people at home. It stressed the importance of hygiene, fresh air, light and quiet. At the time, Florence believed disease was caused by bad smells, the "miasma theory", but she came to accept "germ theory".

## The Nightingale Training School for Nurses

During the Crimean War, a public fund, known as *The Nightingale Fund*, raised £44,000. Florence used it to set up a training school for nurses.

In 1860 Florence established the school at St Thomas' Hospital, Southwark, under the leadership of matron, Sarah Wardroper. Shortly afterwards the hospital relocated temporarily to Surrey Gardens in Chapter Road. Florence helped design the new St Thomas' Hospital, in Lambeth, using the pavilion ward principles, and the school moved again.

The nurses who trained at this school became known as "Nightingales".

## Florence in middle age

In her forties, Florence was frequently very ill, and stayed in bed. She did however carry on working and writing.

Florence was also involved in another Royal Commission – looking at the health of the British army in India. She spent many years campaigning for health and sanitation reforms in India, for the army and later for the population as a whole, although she never visited India.

Florence spent many years in rented accommodation in London. In 1865 her father paid for a lease on a property in South Street, Mayfair. The address then was Number 35, but this was later renumbered to 10 South Street. Florence lived there for the rest of her life.

Florence had many cats during her lifetime, and her book *Notes on Nursing* recommended a small pet as good for patients.

Florence championed many healthcare reforms, including improvements to workhouse infirmaries and maternity wards, known as "lying in wards". She was frequently consulted on hospital design, and the recruitment and training of nurses – both at home and abroad.

## Florence in later life

Florence's father died in 1874, and the two estates, in Derbyshire and Hampshire, were inherited by his sister, Mary, (Mai), and then her son, Florence's cousin, Shore.

By the age of 60, Florence's health had started to improve. She was able to leave her house, and attend social functions. She enjoyed visits to Claydon House, in Buckinghamshire, the home of her sister and brother-in-law.

During her lifetime, Florence received many honours and awards. Queen Victoria presented her with the Nightingale Jewel and Royal Red Cross Medal. She was only the second woman to receive the Freedom of the City of London. And she was the first woman to receive the Order of Merit, from King Edward VII.

## Death and Funeral

Florence died at South Street on 13 August 1910, at the age of 90. As she had instructed, her family declined a funeral at Westminster Abbey, and she was buried at St Margaret's Church, Wellow, in Hampshire. On the day of her funeral, 20 August 1910, a memorial service took place at St Paul's Cathedral.

# A to Z
## of
# FLORENCE
# NIGHTINGALE'S
# LONDON

## 24 Albemarle Street, W1S 4HT

Prince Albert came to the House of Garrard, to commission a brooch known as the Nightingale Jewel, which was given by Queen Victoria to Florence Nightingale in thanks for "her devotion towards the Queen's brave soldiers" in the Crimean War. *See also* National Army Museum, Whitehall.

## Bank of England, Threadneedle Street, EC2R 8AH

Florence was the first woman (apart from the Queen) to feature on a British banknote when she appeared on the £10 note in 1975. Her image was based on two photographs taken for "cartes de visites", small photographs which many people collected in the 1800s, shortly after her return to Britain in 1856.

## 49 Belgrave Square, SW1X 8QZ

This was the London home of Sidney and Elizabeth Herbert. Florence had met them in Rome, and they became close friends. Sidney Herbert was a Member of Parliament. During the Crimean War, he asked Florence to lead a party of nurses to Scutari. Preparing for the journey and recruiting the nurses took place in this house.

## 20 Birchin Lane, EC3V 9DU

Bankers Glyn, Mills & Co were based here in the early 1800s. Florence banked with them during her time in the Crimean War. In 1872, Florence wrote to Glyn, Mills & Co expressing her thanks for "all the kindness you have shown and trouble you have taken - more especially at the time of the Crimean War 1854-6 when I am aware my account with you was a very troublesome customer." Florence's letter is now held in their archives.

## 23 Bloomsbury Square, WC1A 2PJ

This building housed the Headquarters of the Metropolitan and National Nursing Association - founded by Florence Craven (nee Lees) in 1875 for District Nursing, visiting people in their own home. Florence wrote to *The Times* newspaper supporting this association. Florence was godmother to Mrs Craven's first son.

## 50 Bolsover Street, W1W 5NU

In May 1851 Florence and Dr Elizabeth Blackwell went to visit the "spine asylum" or Verral Hospital, named for the surgeon Charles Verral. It was later renamed the National Orthopaedic Hospital. The Royal National Orthopaedic Hospital is now further along Bolsover Street.

## Bolton Street, W1J 8BB

Richard Monckton Milnes, who is generally viewed as Florence's greatest love interest, was born in this street in 1809. As a young woman from a respectable and well-off family, Florence was expected to marry. The couple met in 1842 and had a seven-year courtship. Despite Florence's refusal to marry, the pair remained friends and, as a Member of Parliament, Monckton Milnes would go on to support her work on health reforms.

*Mr Monckton Milnes, MP.*
*Illustration for The Illustrated London*
*News, 19 April 1845*

### British Library, 96 Euston Road, NW1 2DB

The British Library houses most of Florence Nightingale's extensive personal archive as well as many other collections of letters and papers relating to her life and career. It also holds a recording of Florence's voice, in support of the Light Brigade Relief Fund. This recording is also available online. The ill-fated Charge of the Light Brigade took place during the Battle of Balaclava in the Crimean War. It is the subject of a famous poem by Alfred, Lord Tennyson.

### Buckingham Palace, SW1A 1AA

Florence was presented to Queen Victoria here in 1839. She wore a white dress that had been specially bought for the occasion on a trip to Paris.

### 4 Carlton House Terrace, SW1Y 5AH

This was the home of the Prussian Ambassador, Christian von Bunsen, whom Florence met in the early 1840s. He told her about his humanitarian work and the establishment of a German hospital in east London to provide free health care to the German expatriate community. Von Bunsen encouraged Florence to visit both the German Hospital in London and Kaiserswerth in Germany, where she would eventually train as a nurse. *See also* RITSON ROAD.

### 3 Cavendish Place, W1G 9DN

Dr Joseph Clover, anaesthetist, lived here. He anaesthetised Florence in 1871 while the eminent dentist, Edwin Saunders, extracted some teeth. Clover charged two guineas and received a grateful letter from Florence.

## Cavendish Square, W1G 0AN

Florence's parents rented rooms here in 1854. On the morning of 21st October, Florence and her sister, Parthenope, travelled from there to the home of the Herberts on Belgrave Square, before Florence set off for Scutari.

## Chapter Road, SE17 3ES

Pasley Park, formerly known as Royal Surrey Gardens, was used as a pleasure garden. It was also the site of the Surrey Music Hall, the largest venue in London. In August 1856 a celebratory dinner was held there for soldiers returned from the Crimean War, and Florence was guest of honour. In July 1857, a four-day military festival took place, raising funds for Mary Seacole. And from 1862 until 1871 it was the temporary home of St Thomas' Hospital, while its new premises were being built on the Albert Embankment. *See also* ST THOMAS STREET, ST THOMAS' HOSPITAL.

*The temporary St Thomas' Hospital in Royal Surrey Gardens, c.1860s*

## Charles Dickens Museum, 48-9 Doughty Street, WC1N 2LX

The Victorian writer, Charles Dickens, lived here from 1837 to 1851. It is now the Charles Dickens Museum. Dickens and Florence were acquainted. While at this house, he wrote *Martin Chuzzlewit*. One of the book's characters was "Sarah Gamp", a nurse, portrayed as untrained, incompetent and drunk. This was the reputation of nurses at the time. No wonder Florence's family opposed her proposed career.

In 1854 Dickens published an article in the journal *Household Words* entitled *The True Story of The Nuns of Minsk*. One of his sources was "an English Protestant lady", namely Florence. In 1848 in Rome, Florence had met Abbess Makrena Mirazyslawski, a Catholic nun who had suffered persecution by the Russian Orthodox church. Florence had made notes of her interview with the abbess and sent them to Dickens.

## 32 Charlton Place, N1 8AJ

Florence did some fundraising for Caroline Chisholm, philanthropist, known as "The Emigrants' Friend" because of the work she did to assist people emigrating to Australia.

## 12 Chester Street, SW1X 7BB

This was the London home of Douglas Galton and his wife, Marianne (nee Nicholson), a cousin of Florence. They had a room specifically for prints of Florence. Galton was also the architect of the Royal Herbert Hospital, Woolwich. Florence was godmother to their daughter, Gwendolen. *See also* GILBERT CLOSE.

## 9 Chesterfield Street, W1J 5JQ

Florence moved to this "fashionable old maid's house" in March 1862, paid for by her father. It was so filthy, Florence referred to it as the "Pigsty". Her friend Dr Sutherland, physician and sanitation expert, believed if she had not removed the dirty furnishings and bedding, she might have caught typhus.

## 22 College Hill, EC4R 2RP

Florence's solicitors, Janson, Cobb and Pearson, were located here. The entrance is in a courtyard, through the large entrance doors. Florence had consulted the solicitors when drawing up and amending her will. After Florence's death, the firm paid a legacy to Mary Farr, daughter of Dr William Farr, statistician.

## Cork Street, W1S 3HL

The former Burlington Hotel stood here from the 1820s until it was demolished in 1935. The hotel consisted of a collection of houses at 19 Cork Street (main entrance) and 29 and 30 Old Burlington Street. Florence often stayed at the hotel when visiting London, first coming here in 1842 with her family for the "season". *See also* KENSINGTON PALACE. Between 1860

*Burlington Hotel, Cork Street, London.*
*Postcard, early 20th century*

and 1864, Florence lived in a suite of rooms in the hotel. It was here that she wrote both *Notes on Hospitals* and *Notes on Nursing*. She also formed her "Little War Office" here to work on army health reforms. This consisted of Secretary of State for War Sidney Herbert, her brother-in-law Sir Harry Verney MP, her cousin-in-law Arthur Clough, sanitation expert Dr John Sutherland and her aunt Mai Smith. *See also* HOUSES OF PARLIAMENT, PALL MALL.

Never overly impressed with the cleanliness of the hotel, Florence had a constant battle with the staff to improve hygiene standards and referred to it as "the dingy old Burlington".

## 65 Cornhill, EC3V 3NB

This was the location of the book publishers Smith, Elder and Co. In 1859 they published *England and Her Soldiers*, a collaboration between Florence and the writer and journalist, Harriet Martineau. It incorporated Florence's analysis of the statistical data about the Crimean War, and in particular included her diagram of the causes of death. Month by month she showed deaths by preventable disease, wounds and other causes. She called this diagram a "coxcomb", after the top of a cockerel's head. It is also known as a rose or polar area diagram.

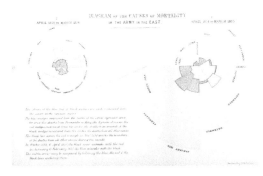

*Florence's "coxcomb" or polar area diagram of the causes of death in the Crimean War*

## 74 Courtfield Gardens, SW5 0NL

This was the home of Lady Alicia Blackwood, who had travelled to the Crimean War with her husband, a chaplain. Her offer to help Florence was treated with caution, as Florence had received such offers from ladies before, and they had come to nothing. But Lady Alicia Blackwood was true to her word, and took charge of the unofficial hospital for the wives and widows of soldiers in Scutari, and their children. She wrote a book about her experiences. The two women remained friends.

## Covent Garden Market, WC2E 8RF

Florence would sometimes walk from Harley Street to Covent Garden market to buy her own vegetables. Her sister did not approve.

## Cromwell Road, SW7 5BD

Hilary Bonham Carter, one of Florence's cousins, was an artist. She exhibited a plaster statuette of Florence at the International Exhibition of 1862, held on the site of what is now the Natural History Museum. Several small copies of the figure were made and presented to friends and other institutions. Florence's mother, unimpressed, said she was "shocked at the poor little finnikin minnikin". There is a copy of this statuette at Claydon House, Buckinghamshire – the former home of Florence's sister, Parthenope.

## Dartmouth Park Hill, N19 5JG

The Highgate Wing of the Whittington Hospital was formerly the St Pancras Workhouse infirmary, or hospital. Originally workhouses included infirmaries, where able-bodied poor women cared for the sick poor. These women were not trained, and the standard of care was low. Florence campaigned for the sick poor to receive professional nursing, preferably in purpose-built infirmaries separate from the workhouses. This infirmary was one of the first to be built separately from its workhouse. Highgate became the home of London's first Poor Law School of Nursing, set up in association with *The Nightingale Fund*. *See also* EUSTON STATION.

## 33 Dean Street, W1D 4PW

This was the home of Dr Joseph Rogers, health care reformer and medical officer for the Cleveland Street Workhouse. He and some of his fellow medical professionals set up a pressure group called the Association for the Improvement of the Infirmaries of London Workhouses. This organisation attracted some influential members, including Florence, Charles Dickens, and Louisa Twining of the tea family.

## 31 Dover Street, W1S 4ND

The site of Peary's Hotel is where Florence stayed for a while in early 1862. Whilst here, she suffered a severe attack of Crimean Fever, a bacterial infection she had previously contracted in the Crimea. Florence was so ill that she amended her will. In it, she requested that her body be left to medical science, a request that her family could not bring themselves to comply with when she died in 1910. *See also* WELLCOME COLLECTION.

## 10 Downing Street, SW1A 2AA

In 1882, Prime Minister, William Gladstone, invited Florence to attend a Royal Review of Returning Troops from Egypt, taking place on Horse Guards Parade. They sat on a raised platform in the garden of Number 10.

## Euston Station, NW1 2HS

Florence was travelling back to London by train from Claydon House, Buckinghamshire, when her Persian kitten "Quiz" jumped out of the window at Watford. Florence summoned help from the stationmasters and the kitten was found unhurt. It spent the night at the Euston Station Parcels Office.

In 1848 WH Smith & Son opened the first ever travel retail store in Euston station. With the growth of the railway network, other station bookstalls followed. WH Smith & Son placed 1,000 leaflets for *The Nightingale Fund* on their station bookstalls. *See also* Hyde Park Gardens.

## 85 Fleet Street, EC4Y 1AE

A previous building on this site housed the offices of the satirical magazine *Punch*, which was founded by Henry Mayhew and Ebenezer Landells in 1841 and was known for its humorous political comment. Florence featured in cartoons during the Crimean War period and not always in a good way. Despite this, in 1856, *Punch* proposed a statue to honour Florence's work in the war.

## 169 Fleet Street, EC4A 2EA

This used to be the offices of publisher Seeley, Burnside and Seeley. In 1834 they published a book by American theologian, Jacob Abbott, entitled *The Corner-stone; or, A Familiar Illustration of the Principles of Christian Truth*. Florence read the book in 1836 and credited it with her conversion. Driven by her faith, Florence went on to receive her "calling from God" in 1837.

## Floris, 89 Jermyn Street, SW1Y 6JH

Florence was a customer of Floris, and her two favourite scents, Night Scented Jasmine and White Rose, are still available for purchase today. The shop has a small museum, where a letter from Florence Nightingale, written in 1863, is on display.

*Letter to Floris from Florence dated 20 July 1863 with a bottle of perfume*

*Jar of beef extract, which is still sold by Fortnum & Mason*

## Fortnum & Mason, 181 Piccadilly, W1A 1ER

When she was working at Harley Street, Florence improved the food supply. She wrote in one of her quarterly reports, "I now lay in groceries monthly from Fortnum and Mason".

During the Crimean War many people sent packages and gifts for the wounded soldiers. Queen Victoria ordered Fortnum & Mason to "despatch without delay" 250lbs of beef tea to Florence to help the injured and wounded in Scutari Hospital.

## Gilbert Close, SE18 4PR

This private residential development was formerly a military hospital. It was built in 1865 and was initially called the Herbert Hospital, after Sidney Herbert, MP. It was later renamed the Royal Herbert Hospital. The architect was Douglas Galton, an accomplished engineer, married to Florence's cousin, Marianne (nee Nicholson). It was built according to the pavilion design for wards favoured by Florence.

## 14 Gordon Square, WC1H 0AR

Following her birth at the Villa la Colombaia in the Italian city of Florence on 12 May 1820, the family maid Fanny Gale was sent back to England to register Florence's birth at Dr Williams's Library. Florence's family were Unitarians, so her birth was recorded in the Protestant Dissenters Register.

*Florence's birth certificate*

## 47 Gower Street, WC1E 6HG

Jerry Barrett painted *The Mission of Mercy: Florence Nightingale Receiving the Wounded at Scutari* in his studio. He had travelled out to Scutari to create preliminary sketches but failed to get Florence to agree to sit for him. Many of the people featured in the painting sat for him in his London studio upon their return to England. Florence's mother, Fanny, came to the studio to see the painting, but Florence is not known to have visited as she rarely consented to having her portrait painted or photographs taken. *See also* NATIONAL PORTRAIT GALLERY.

## 6-7 Great Newport Street, WC2H 7JB

In January 1929 Reginald Berkeley's play, *The Lady with a Lamp*, opened at the Arts Theatre, telling the story of Florence Nightingale, and starring Edith Evans. It transferred to the Garrick Theatre on Charing Cross Road. It also played for 12 performances on Broadway, New York.

## Guildhall, Guildhall Yard, EC2V 7HH

In 1908, Florence was awarded the Honorary Freedom of the City of London – only the second woman to receive it, the first being philanthropist Angela Burdett-Coutts in 1872.

*Certificate of Honorary Freedom of the City of London bestowed on Florence*
*13 February 1908*

*Oak casket holding*
*Florence's Honorary Freedom*
*of the City of London*

Instead of the usual gold casket, at her request, Florence's Freedom was presented in an oak casket and 100 guineas was donated to the Establishment for Gentlewomen. Florence's cousin, Louis Shore Nightingale, accepted the honour on her behalf, as she was bedridden at the time. Florence's Freedom certificate can be seen at the Florence Nightingale Museum.

## 90 Harley Street, W1G 7HS

This is the site of the former Establishment for Gentlewomen during Illness, a private hospital. In 1853, Florence was appointed as the Lady Superintendent, at the time an unpaid role. She brought about many improvements to the running of the hospital and instigated quarterly reports to the governors. She remained there until 1854. An inscription on the front of the building states that Florence Nightingale left the hospital for the Crimea on 21 October 1854. The successor organisation moved to Lisson Grove and is now called the Nightingale Hospital.

*Fire screen that Florence used to make her rooms in the hospital more homely. Screens were used to protect a lady's complexion from the effects of heat from a fireplace*

## Hampstead

Between 1859 and 1862 Florence spent periods of time in Hampstead, to escape from city life, and to experience a change of scenery. She received many visitors – colleagues, friends and relatives. She stayed at 105 Frognal, 7 Oak Hill Park and 3 Upper Terrace. However, she decided the area was too damp and cold for a permanent home.

*Carriage used by Florence to travel around in the Crimea*

## Harrods, 87 Brompton Road, SW1X 7XL

The carriage used by Florence in the Crimea was displayed in Harrods in 1950 to promote Cecil Woodham-Smith's biography of her. The carriage had previously belonged to Prince Menschikov, Commander-in-Chief of the Russian forces on land and sea.

In 1856, the carriage had been presented to Florence by Colonel William McMurdo of the Land Transport Corps in the Crimea. After the end of the war, the chef Alexis Soyer arranged for it to be returned to England. In 1930 it was presented to the Nightingale Training School for Nurses at St Thomas' Hospital, where the nurses nicknamed it "Florrie's Lorry". It now belongs to the Florence Nightingale Museum and is located at Claydon House, in Buckinghamshire, formerly the country home of Florence's sister, Parthenope, and her husband, Sir Harry Verney.

## 283 Harrow Road, W9 3RN

This was originally the site of a medieval leper hospital, but from 1842 until its closure in 1952 this was the London Lock Hospital, which was a centre for the treatment of venereal disease. Its name derives from the rags or "locks" that were used to cover the sores of leper patients in the medieval lock hospitals. Florence visited the Lock Hospital in 1851 with her friend, Dr Elizabeth Blackwell, who had become the first woman to qualify as a doctor in the USA and who, at the time, was working at St Bartholomew's Hospital.

## Houses of Parliament, SW1A 0AA

Florence was very familiar with the workings of Parliament, not only through her work on health reforms in later life but also through her family's political careers. Her grandfather, William Smith, was a radical Member of Parliament (MP) who worked with William Wilberforce on the abolition of slavery. Her brother-in-law, Sir Harry Verney, was known in Parliament as "the Member for Miss Nightingale", and some of her cousins were Liberal MPs. Her own father also, unsuccessfully, stood for election to the Liberal Party.

Florence's own political affiliations were with the Liberal Party. However, she worked closely with politicians of all parties to achieve health reforms. One such was Robert Loyd-Lindsay, later Baron Wantage, who she worked alongside to establish the National Aid Society, which was the forerunner to the British Red Cross.

In 1868 Florence worked on the Royal Sanitary Commission and lobbied MP James Stansfeld, the minister responsible, to strengthen the Public Health Act. This 1848 act had been introduced to improve sanitation in homes through the creation and repair of sewers to combat the spread of disease. Florence also collaborated with sanitary reformer Edwin Chadwick. It was Chadwick who encouraged Florence to write up her research on sanitation and health care, which was published as her book *Notes on Nursing*. *See also* Cork Street, Pall Mall.

Florence supported many political campaigns, including one to repeal the Contagious Diseases Act. This Act gave the police powers to arrest any woman suspected of prostitution, forced women to undergo invasive examinations for venereal disease and, if declared infected, be detained in a locked hospital. Florence's use of statistics on hospital admissions linked to venereal disease showed that this type of regulation did not reduce cases. *See also* North View, Upper Berkeley Street.

## Hyde Park, W2 2UH

Later in life, when Florence's health had improved, she would take carriage drives around Hyde Park.

## 34 Hyde Park Gardens, W2 2TX

This was the home (now demolished) of Charles and Selina Bracebridge in 1851. They were close friends of Florence and travelled extensively with her, to Rome, Greece, Egypt, France and Germany. Selina Bracebridge was an artist and travel writer. Florence was very close to her, and described her as "my more than mother".

Selina Bracebridge helped Florence to recruit the first party of nurses for the Crimean War. Both the Bracebridges travelled to Scutari with Florence's party and stayed for several months. Selina Bracebridge was put in charge of the Free Gift Store – looking after items sent out to Florence by members of the public. Charles

Bracebridge served as a trustee of *The Nightingale Fund. See also* Hyde Park Square.

## 5 Hyde Park Square, W2 2NL

Henry Bonham Carter, a cousin of Florence, lived here with his family. The house has been demolished. For more than 50 years he served as the secretary of *The Nightingale Fund Council*. Initially he and Florence wrote letters to each other. Florence was reluctant to see anyone in person, and carried out her business by correspondence. When her cousin moved here, he was able to walk to Florence's home in South Street, and persuaded her to see him. He was also an executor of Florence's will. *See also* King Street.

## Kensington Palace, Kensington Gardens, W8 4PX

In the 1860s, Queen Victoria offered Florence an apartment in Kensington Palace. She declined as she preferred to reside at the Burlington Hotel which was more centrally located. *See also* Cork Street.

## 26 King Street, SW1Y 6QW

In 1855, the inaugural meeting of *The Nightingale Fund* was held at Willis's Rooms, a suite of Assembly Rooms used for balls, concerts, dinners and public meetings, which were located here. A national appeal to recognise Florence's work in the Crimean War, the fund was so well supported by the public that it raised over £44,000 (*see poster overleaf*). Florence used the money to start her School of Nursing, the first professional secular school of nursing in the world. *See also* Parliament Street.

THE

# NIGHTINGALE
## FUND.

THE signal services rendered by Miss NIGHTINGALE, to the sick and wounded of the British Forces in the East, have excited throughout the Country a universal desire to testify by some marked and substantial acknowledgment, the gratitude and admiration of the British people.

But Miss NIGHTINGALE has nobly refused to accept any testimonial from which she could derive personal advantage of any description; while it is ascertained that the tribute most in harmony with her feelings and wishes, would be to afford further scope for her disinterested exertions by placing under her immediate superintendance the establishment of an Institution for the reception, protection, and training, of Hospital Nurses and Assistants, whereby the inestimable blessings of the system she has introduced, may be perpetuated and extended generally to the Poor, who may be suffering from sickness or accident.

To effect this object a public appeal has been made, to which the noble, the wealthy, and the benevolent, have liberally responded. But it is felt, that opportunity should not be denied to any class to manifest the sympathy all are known to entertain towards their devoted and highminded Countrywoman. The contributions, however small, of those who are dependent upon their labor, will have a peculiar fitness when given for an object by which the necessitous are to be exclusively benefited; while it is certain the widow's mite will have equal value in the estimation of Miss NIGHTINGALE, with the largest gifts of the great and the affluent.

Partaking in these views, the Proprietors of this Establishment have given permission for a Subscription Book to be opened in the Counting House where any contributions however small, will be received and recorded; and the amount collected will be transmitted to the Committee and advertised as the contribution of the Workmen and others in this Establishment.

*December 28th 1855.*

*Poster displayed in 1855 to appeal for contributions "however small" to The Nightingale Fund*

## King Charles Street, SW1A 2AH

The former India Office is on this street. About half way along the street on the right-hand side, from Whitehall, is an entrance into the building. Towards the top of the building is a frieze, showing animals from the sub-continent, including oxen, lions and elephants.

From 1857, for about 40 years Florence campaigned on various matters relating to sanitation, health and welfare reform in India. Initially, her interest was in the British Army in India, but she later turned her attention to the whole country, investigating famine relief, irrigation, land tenure, and the education of women. She campaigned for reform over many years, and wrote papers, observations, newspaper articles and reports for conferences.

Although at first Florence's outlook was rather imperialist, over time her view changed and she advocated self-government by the Indian people. Florence never visited the country, but carried out her campaigning by correspondence. She owned two irrigation maps of India, bought from Stanfords travel bookshop, and which she specifically mentioned in her will. *See also* MERCER WALK.

## 35-43 Lincoln's Inn Fields, WC2A 3PE

Florence visited the museum of the Royal College of Surgeons with Selina Bracebridge, in 1847. The museum is known as the Hunterian, after the 18th century surgeon and anatomist, John Hunter.

## London Bridge station, Station Approach Road, Southwark, SE1 9SP

This was the starting point for the journey to Scutari. Florence, the Bracebridges and the nurses travelled to the Kent coast by rail, crossed the channel by steamer, and then journeyed by rail to Paris. By rail and boat they travelled to Marseilles, where they boarded the P&O steamer *Vectis*, bound for Constantinople (Istanbul).

## Lord Raglan Pub, St Martins le Grand, EC1A 4ER

The pub is named for Fitzroy Somerset, 1st Baron Raglan, who was commander of the British troops in the Crimean War. When Florence became ill with Crimean Fever in May 1855 and hovered on the brink of death, the troops waited with bated breath for her recovery and Lord Raglan travelled to visit her. On his arrival at her medical hut, Lord Raglan was initially refused entrance by Mrs Roberts, who was tending Florence, as she didn't recognise him. When challenged as to who he was, he told Mrs Roberts that he was "only a soldier but I have ridden a long way, and your patient knows me very well". When Florence recovered from her fever, the soldiers and the nation breathed a huge sigh of relief.

## Mary Seacole statue, St Thomas' Hospital, Westminster Bridge Road, SE1 7EH

Outside St Thomas' Hospital is a larger-than-life size bronze statue of Mary Seacole by Martin Jennings, unveiled in 2016. Mary Seacole was born in Jamaica in 1805 of British and Jamaican heritage. From her mother, a "doctress", she learnt healing and nursing skills. Mrs Seacole applied to work as a nurse in the Crimean War, but Florence had already left and she was turned down by the organising committee. She made her own way to the Crimean Peninsula, staying overnight at Scutari, where she met Florence.

At her establishment, the British Hotel, she served food and beverages, and provided accommodation. She also dispensed medications and provided nursing skills. After the Crimean War, she was declared bankrupt. A support fund was set up, and many prominent people donated to it, including Florence. There is a portrait of Mary Seacole in the National Portrait Gallery, by AC Challen. There is also a blue plaque to her at 14 Soho Square and a green plaque at 147 George Street, Marylebone.

## 7 Mercer Walk, WC2H 9FA

Stanfords, the specialist travel and map bookshop, hold in their archives an original letter from Florence, thanking them for mounting two irrigation maps of India. These precious maps were mentioned in Florence's will. *See also* KING CHARLES STREET.

*Letter from Florence to Stanfords dated 13 November 1884*

## National Army Museum, Royal Hospital Road, SW3 4HT

The National Army Museum holds a number of honours that were awarded to Florence. These include the Nightingale Jewel awarded to her by Queen Victoria in 1855, the Royal Red Cross awarded in 1883, the Order of the Hospital of St John of Jerusalem in England awarded in 1904 and the Order of Merit awarded by King Edward VII in 1907. Following her death, Florence specifically wanted her awards to be displayed in a place where soldiers could see them. *See also* ALBEMARLE STREET, WHITEHALL.

*Jewel decorated with a red cross and three stars given by Queen Victoria to Florence Nightingale for her work in Crimea. Lithograph, 14 February 1856*

## National Portrait Gallery, St Martin's Place, WC2H 0HE

The National Portrait Gallery acquired both of artist Jerry Barrett's Crimean War paintings at auction in 1993 and the two are usually displayed together. In 1855, Barrett painted *Queen Victoria's First Visit to her Wounded Soldiers*. Barrett travelled out to the Crimean War in 1856 to paint *The Mission of Mercy: Florence Nightingale Receiving the Wounded at Scutari*.

Barrett drew a number of preliminary sketches to capture the the scene at Scutari hospital and form the outline of his painting. However, he completely failed to persuade Florence to sit for him and only managed to sketch a headshot of her as she walked through the harbour the day before her departure back to England.

The painting was completed at Barrett's London studio and Florence is instantly recognisable, wearing her familiar uniform of a dark dress and white lace cap. The painting features a number of key figures, including her friends Charles and Selina Bracebridge and three of the original 38 nurses: Mrs Roberts, Reverend Mother Mary Clare Moore and Miss Sarah Tebbut. The gallery has a full key of who is who on its website. *See also* GOWER STREET.

*The Mission of Mercy: Florence Nightingale receiving the Wounded at Scutari by Jerry Barrett. Oil on canvas, 1857*

### 8 North View, SW19 4UJ

In the early 1890s, social reformer Josephine Butler lived here with her son following the death of her husband. Butler was Secretary to the Ladies' National Association for the Repeal of the Contagious Diseases Acts, a campaign that Florence was prominent in. There is a blue plaque to Butler on the house. *See also* Houses of Parliament.

### 10/11 Observatory Gardens, W8 7HY

Florence was interested in astronomy. In 1843 she visited Sir James South, one of the founders of the Royal Astronomical Society. In the garden of his home, he had had an observatory constructed, where Florence observed the stars and planets. Here she met and became friends with Angela Burdett-Coutts, a wealthy philanthropist. The blue plaque on the railings explains the origins of the name Observatory Gardens.

### 10 Osnaburgh Street, NW1 3DE

Priscilla Lydia Sellon founded an Anglican sisterhood in Devonport, Plymouth, in 1848. They became known as the Devonport Sisters of Mercy, or Sellonites. Eight of these sisters accompanied Florence to Scutari. They had valuable nursing experience, gained during a cholera outbreak. In 1856, the Sisters combined with another order to form the Society of the Holy Trinity, led by Miss Sellon. They established a convalescent hospital, St Saviour's, at 10 Osnaburgh Street, now demolished.

### 1 Our Lady's Close, SE19 3FA

Our Lady of Fidelity, a Roman Catholic convent, sent five nuns to Scutari with Florence in October 1854. Before the Crimean War they were looking after orphans, and had no direct experience of nursing wounded soldiers. They returned to England in December 1854.

### 309 Oxford Street, W1C 2DX

Lizzie Caswall Smith, photographer, had a studio here. In 1910 she took a black and white photograph of Florence, in South Street. It is possibly the last photograph ever taken of her. On the back of the photograph Caswall Smith wrote "Florence Nightingale taken just before she died, House near Park Lane (London). The only photograph I ever took out of studio – I shall never forget the experience."

### 59 Pall Mall, SW1Y 5JH

The first edition of Florence's book, *Notes on Nursing: What it is, and what it is not* was published in 1859 by Harrison and Sons.

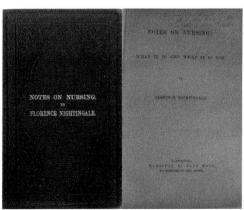

*The earliest known copy of Florence's international bestselling book,* Notes on Nursing. *Inside it is inscribed by Florence and dated New Year's Day 1860*

They described themselves as "Bookseller to the Queen". This short book, which has never been out of print, was not intended to be a training manual for nurses. It was meant to "give hints for thought to women who have personal charge of the health of others." It included chapters on ventilation and warming, noise, food, light, cleanliness and the observation of the sick. *See also* Cork Street, Houses of Parliament.

## 89 Pall Mall, SW1Y 5HS

The War Office, a government department, opened here in 1858. Sidney Herbert served as the Secretary of State for War from 1859 until his death in 1861. He and Florence campaigned to reform the War Office. The Royal Automobile Club now stands on the site. After the death of Sidney Herbert, a statue of him by J.H. Foley was erected outside the building. It was later moved to Waterloo Place, alongside the statue of Florence.

## 104 Pall Mall, SW1Y 5EW

The Reform Club, a private members' club, employed two notable chefs. Alexis Soyer worked there from 1837 to 1850. He volunteered his services to help with the Crimean War, travelled to Scutari and re-organised the hospital catering. He developed a stove for military use, which was in use for over a century. Examples are in the Florence Nightingale Museum and the National Army Museum. There is a green plaque to him at 28 Marlborough Rd, St John's Wood.

Charles Francatelli, at the Reform Club from 1854 to 1861, developed a recipe for "rice a la soeur Nightingale", fish with spiced rice, in honour of Florence, who was known to be fond of curry.

## 107 Pall Mall, SW1Y 5ER

Florence's father, William Edward Nightingale, was a member of the Athenaeum, a private gentlemen's club, which was founded in 1824. Florence's friend and cousin in law, Arthur Clough was also a member and Lord Palmerston, who knew the Nightingales, was a founding member.

## Park Street, W1K 7LQ

The film star, Dame Anna Neagle (born Florence Marjorie Robertson), and her film producer husband, Herbert Wilcox, lived from 1950 until 1964 in the top floor flat of Aldford House, on the corner of Park Street and South Street. The 1951 film *The Lady with a Lamp*, produced and directed by Wilcox, starred Anna Neagle as Florence. There is a green plaque to them both on the South Street side of the building.

When Florence was in Athens in 1850, she rescued an owl, which she called "Athena". Sadly, it died before she left for Scutari, and the owl was stuffed. During her research for the film, Anna Neagle re-discovered the stuffed owl in Mayfair. "Athena" now resides at the Florence Nightingale Museum.

## Parkers Row, SE1 2DQ

Five of the original 38 women who arrived in Scutari with Florence came from this Roman Catholic Convent of Mercy. Three more nuns followed in 1856. Florence formed a lifelong friendship with Reverend Mother Mary Clare Moore. Florence stopped off at the convent in Bermondsey on her way home from the Crimean War. Four of the Bermondsey sisters were awarded the Royal Red Cross medal by Queen Victoria. There is a small heritage centre at

the convent, containing information about the sisters, and correspondence with Florence.

## Parliament Square, SW1P 3BD

Parliament Square contains statues of many notable statesmen,
not just from Britain but from around the world, including some
that Florence knew in her lifetime.

Henry John Temple, 3rd Viscount Palmerston, was a friend of
the Nightingales. His country estate, Broadlands, was close to Florence's family home of Embley Park in Hampshire. Palmerston was
Home Secretary at the start of the Crimean War and was a strong
advocate for Britain entering the war. He also sent a "Sanitary
Commission" out to Scutari Hospital to help alleviate the horrific
conditions. Florence fully supported the Commission and often
referred to Palmerston as a "true gentleman".

Benjamin Disraeli, 1st Earl of Beaconsfield, served as Prime
Minister twice, in 1868 and from 1874 to 1880. Although Florence
did not particularly like him, Disraeli was a great reformer and built
on Florence's work on sanitation, introducing a new Public Health
Act in 1875. This included the appointment of Medical Officers of
Health.

Lawyer and leading Indian Independence campaigner, Mahatma Gandhi was a great admirer of Florence. He wrote a tribute to
her in the newspaper *Indian Opinion* in 1905, praising her selfless-
ness and "miraculous" reductions of death rates at Scutari Hospital.
Florence was a supporter of self-government in India and worked
from her home in London to improve health, education and
sanitary conditions in India. *See also* KING CHARLES STREET.

## 5 Parliament Street, SW1A 2LZ

In 1855, rooms on the first floor served as offices of *The Nightingale Fund*. The fund raised over £44,000 and *The Nightingale Fund Council* still exists today. *See also* QUEEN VICTORIA STREET.

## 2 Pearson Square, Fitzroy Place, W1T 3BF

The Fitzrovia Chapel, by architect John Loughborough Pearson, was formerly the chapel for the Middlesex Hospital. In 1854 London experienced a severe cholera outbreak, and Florence took leave from Harley Street to superintend the victims at the Middlesex Hospital. The chapel is all that remains of the hospital.

## 16 Queen Anne's Gate, SW1H 9AA

The eastern part of this street was previously known as Park Street, and Florence's maternal grandparents, William and Frances Smith, had a London home at 6 Park Street, now 16 Queen Anne's Gate.

## 12 Queen Square, WC1N 3AR

This building was built in 1906 for St John's House – a Protestant religious community founded in 1848 as a training institution for nurses for hospitals, families and the poor. There is a statue of St John above the entrance, and two plaques at first floor level record the name and dates of St John's House. Six St John's nurses accompanied Florence to Scutari. One of those nurses, Elizabeth Drake, died of fever at Balaclava in the Crimea in August 1855.

## 130 Queen Victoria Street, EC4V 4BT

The College of Arms's main role is to grant coats of arms, however Florence's father never applied for one. Florence's father was born William Edward Shore but changed his last name to Nightingale in 1815, as a condition of inheriting the estate of his great uncle Peter Nightingale. This was done by the granting of a royal licence at the College of Arms, as was the custom at the time.

## 160 Queen Victoria Street, EC4V 4LA

The office block stands on the former site of *The Times* newspaper. The newspaper did more than just reporting on the Crimean War. They set up *The Times Fund*, receiving public donations. Florence used this fund, as well as government funding, to purchase supplies for the hospitals in Scutari.

When John Macdonald, *The Times Fund* manager who had worked with Florence in Scutari, returned home, he wrote a famous piece for the newspaper, describing Florence as a "ministering angel", portraying her as "...alone, with a little lamp in her hand, making her solitary rounds." The image of Florence as "the lady with the lamp" caught the public's attention, and has persisted to this day.

Even before the end of the Crimean War, an appeal was launched to raise funds by public subscription, in honour of Florence. This would become *The Nightingale Fund*. *The Times* carried subscription lists and reports of meetings. *See also* St Thomas Street.

## Randolph Avenue, W9

Dr William Farr, statistician and epidemiologist, lived on this road. He worked closely with Florence on health and army sanitary reforms, serving on the commission set up after the Crimean War, and later on the Sanitary Commission for India. As a member of the Statistical Society of London (later Royal Statistical Society) he proposed Florence for membership. She became the first female fellow in 1858. Dr Farr named his youngest daughter Florence. In later life he made some unwise investments. Florence contributed to a fund set up to provide for his unmarried daughters. *See also* ST JAMES'S SQUARE.

## Ritson Road, E8 1DF

This was the site of the former German Hospital, which opened in 1845 to provide care for the German-speaking community in Dalston. At the suggestion of the Prussian Ambassador, Christian von Bunsen, Florence visited in June 1846 with her friends, Charles and Selina Bracebridge. Florence also visited in 1851 with her friend, Dr Elizabeth Blackwell, the first woman to qualify as a doctor in the United States. *See also* CARLTON HOUSE TERRACE.

The original building was demolished, but new buildings from 1863 onwards still stand. The hospital closed in 1987. The buildings are now used for private housing.

*The German Hospital, Dalston, London: seen from the street. Coloured lithograph by Paul Gauci, 1846*

## Royal Courts of Justice, Strand, WC2A 2LL

Florence attended the opening of the Royal Courts of Justice in December 1882 at the invitation of Queen Victoria. The architect was George Edmund Street, who had died before the building was completed.

### Royal Hospital, Royal Hospital Road, SW3 4SR

Some of the soldiers who fought in the Crimean War spent their last days living as "Chelsea Pensioners" in the Royal Hospital Chelsea, a retirement home for army veterans. Florence is known to have provided a work reference for one veteran and, when she died in 1910, some of the Chelsea Pensioners of the Crimean War attended her memorial service at St Paul's Cathedral.

### Royal London Hospital, Whitechapel Road, E1 1FR

*Copy of a minute of the Court of Governors of the London Hospital, making Florence an Honorary Life Governor, March 1856*

This large teaching hospital was formerly known as the London Hospital. In March 1856 the Court of Governors resolved to make Florence an Honorary Life Governor, in recognition of her work with the British Forces in the Crimean War. A bound copy of the Annual Report was prepared for presentation to Florence, incorporating a handwritten copy of the minute of the meeting. She wrote a letter of thanks from Scutari. She visited the hospital in December 1856, and wrote in the Visitors Book "I have just visited this hospital and can truly say how admirable I consider its arrangements.".

In 1880 Eva Luckes was appointed matron. She and Florence corresponded over many years, particularly on the subject of the state registration of nurses, which neither of them agreed with.

## 28 St Ann's Street, SW1P 2DE

In Victorian times there was a Ragged School here. Education was expensive, so several philanthropists set up "Ragged Schools" for poor children, and recruited volunteers as teachers. In 1849 Florence volunteered as a teacher, and enjoyed spending time with her "little thieves in Westminster".

In 1850, Florence wrote an English language pamphlet about the Kaiserswerth hospital in Germany. It was printed by the London Ragged Colonial Training School at 28 St Ann's Street. The building no longer survives.

## St Bartholomew's Hospital, West Smithfield, EC1A 7BE

Florence was familiar with the hospital as her own doctor, Dr James Paget, worked here. She also met Dr Elizabeth Blackwell here, who worked alongside Dr Paget in 1850, having become the first woman to qualify as a doctor in the USA. Florence and Dr Blackwell became friends and remained so throughout their lives, both passing away in 1910.

## St James's Square, SW1Y 4LG

Florence rented rooms in this square in 1853 when she was Superintendent of the Establishment for Gentlewomen during Illness and would come here at weekends when she was not on duty. *See also* HARLEY STREET.

## 12 St James's Square, SW1Y 4LB

This was the home of Augusta Ada King, Countess of Lovelace, who is generally known as Ada Lovelace. Florence and Lovelace were friends and shared a love of mathematics and statistics. Lovelace died aged only 36 and Florence wrote "They said she could not possibly have lived so long, were it not for the tremendous vitality of the brain, that would not die."

*Certificate nominating Florence as a Fellow of the Statistical Society of London in 1858. The lead signature is that of William Farr*

## 14 St James's Square, SW1Y 4LG

Florence was a member of the London Library, a private lending library, which was established in 1841. However, she cancelled her membership as she never used it.

In the 1850s, the London Library was also home to the London Statistical Society. Florence's work, collating and analysing data on the causes of mortality during the Crimean War, led to her being the first female to be elected to the Society. She remained a member from 1858 until her death in 1910. Today it is known as the Royal Statistical Society.

Jointly with the Health Foundation charity, they recognise the achievements of practitioners in applied healthcare data analytics through the Florence Nightingale Award for Excellence in Healthcare Data Analytics.

## St Margaret's Church, St Margaret Street, SW1P 3JX

St Margaret's Church is where Florence's parents, William Edward Nightingale and Frances (Fanny) Smith married on 1 June

1818. It was also where nurse Isabel Adams Hampton married Dr Hunter Robb in 1894, with the bride carrying a wedding bouquet provided by Florence. Hampton was the first Superintendent of Nurses and the Principal of the Johns Hopkins School of Nursing in Baltimore, USA. In 1893 Hampton arranged for Florence to send a paper on nursing the sick to the International Congress of Charities, Correction and Philanthropy in Chicago.

## 11 St Mark's Crescent, NW1 7TS

This was the home of Arthur Hugh Clough from 1854-1859, who was part of Florence's "Little War Office", working with her on health reforms. Clough was married to Florence's cousin, Blanche Shore Smith, the daughter of her Aunt Mai. In 1856, Clough was appointed secretary to a commission to study the education and training of military personnel in other countries. Thus, he was well placed to work alongside Florence on her army health reforms. Florence's devoted assistant, Clough worked tirelessly to support her but sadly became ill. Whilst on a trip to improve his health, he contracted malaria and died in the city of Florence in 1861. There is a blue plaque on the house commemorating him.

## St Paul's Cathedral, EC4M 8AD

When Florence died on 13 August 1910, she had left strict instructions not to have any fuss at her funeral, so she was buried at St Margaret's Church near the family home, Embley Park, in Hampshire. However, on the same day as her funeral took place, 20 August, a memorial service was held at St Paul's Cathedral. There was a congregation of over 3,000 people, including hundreds of nurses from civilian and military hospitals and delegations from the British Red Cross, Salvation Army, and the Indian Medical Service among others. In pride of place were 40 veterans of the Crimea, some of whom were Chelsea Pensioners.

In the crypt there is a memorial to Florence sculpted by Arthur George Walker, which was unveiled by Queen Mary in 1917.

*Nurses arriving at St Paul's Cathedral for Florence's memorial service, 20 August 1910*

### 9a St Thomas Street, SE1 9RY

The Old Operating Theatre Museum and Herb Garret was originally the chapel of the medieval St Thomas' Hospital. St Thomas' Hospital was still located here in 1860 when Florence founded her School of Nursing at the hospital using money raised from *The Nightingale Fund. See also* STRAND.

The first nurses began their training on 9th July under the school's first head, Mrs Sarah Wardroper, who was matron at the hospital. Training lasted one year. When they graduated, the nurses, known as Nightingales, had a chance to meet Florence either at her South Street home or at Claydon House, the country home of her sister and brother-in-law. Although Florence didn't teach at the school, she kept fully up to date with the students' progress and wrote extensive notes on all of them. Many of Florence's "Nightingale nurses" went on to become matrons or superintendents in other hospitals and in workhouse infirmaries.

The nursing school moved with the hospital to temporary premises in Royal Surrey Gardens at Pasley Park in 1862, and then to the new St Thomas' Hospital that was built in 1871 in Lambeth. The school still exists today as the Florence Nightingale Faculty of Nursing, Midwifery and Palliative Care at King's College London. *See also* Chapter Road, St Thomas' Hospital, Waterloo Road.

## St Thomas' Hospital, Westminster Bridge Road, SE1 7EH

Although St Thomas' Hospital was founded in the late 12th century in Borough, this hospital was built in the 19th century. Florence was heavily involved in the design of the new hospital and corresponded with architects, engineers, doctors, philanthropists and politicians on the matter. The lead architect was Henry Currey and it was built in the pavilion design that Florence favoured. It had 588 beds and wards which were 120 feet long, 28 feet wide and 16 feet high. In between the pavilions were courtyards to allow the healing power of fresh air and sunlight in. Queen Victoria opened the new hospital in 1871.

This new pavilion design was much admired and copied, not just across the UK for both civilian and military hospitals, but across the world and there are "Nightingale" design hospitals as far afield as the USA and Australia.

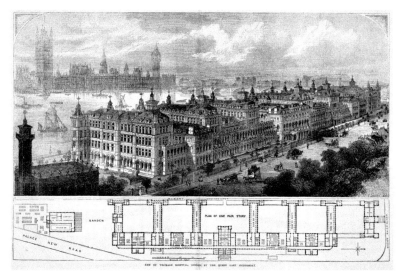

*Plan of the new St Thomas' Hospital in the pavilion design favoured by Florence*

The modern building that houses the main entrance today is the result of rebuilding following bomb damage in World War Two but some of the original pavilions remain. The hospital chapel has a bust of Florence, a memorial to Sarah Wardroper, the first Superintendent of the Nightingale Training School for Nurses, and one to the hospital's architect, Henry Currey. On the ground floor of the hospital is an exhibition on the history of St Thomas' Hospital and a statue of Florence. *See also* CHAPTER ROAD, ST THOMAS STREET, WATERLOO ROAD.

Outside the hospital is a statue of Mary Seacole. *See also* MARY SEACOLE.

## 10 South Street, W1K 1DF

Florence spent the last 45 years of her life living here, from October 1865 until her death in August 1910. Number 4 South Street was the London home of her sister, Parthenope, and her husband, Sir Harry Verney MP and Florence often stayed with them there before she had a permanent home of her own. At Parthenope's persuasion, their father paid £7,000 for a 21-year lease on number 10, so that Florence could be settled.

Florence spent most of her time living in her second-floor bedroom and sitting room, where she had a lovely view across Park Lane to Hyde Park. She lived alone, apart from her servants and her multiple cats. Florence is thought to have had approximately 60 cats over her lifetime and they were her constant companions. She named many of her cats after famous people, including Gladstone, Disraeli and Mr Bismarck, and some after institutions, as there was a Tom for St Thomas' Hospital. Her servants included a cook and her lady's maid, Ellen Kate Tugby. Florence spent her days corresponding with family, friends, politicians and nursing staff and students, and campaigning for health reforms. When well enough, Florence received a steady flow of visitors.

On 30 July 1890, Florence was visited by Colonel Gouraud, from the Thomas Edison Company. He took a recording of her voice on a wax cylinder in support of the Light Brigade Relief Fund, capturing it for posterity. Florence's message to her old comrades can still be heard today and she says: "When I am no longer even a memory, just a name, I hope my voice may perpetuate the great work of my life. God bless my dear old comrades of Balaclava and bring them safe to shore. Florence Nightingale." *See also* BRITISH LIBRARY.

Florence passed away in her bedroom on the afternoon of 13 August 1910 at the age of 90. Her death certificate was certified by

Louisa Garrett Anderson who, like her mother Elizabeth Garrett Anderson, was a doctor.

*Photo of Florence in her bedroom taken by Lizzie Caswall-Smith shortly before Florence died aged 90*

There is a blue plaque on number 10 to commemorate Florence's residence, which was unveiled in 1955 by the then Princess Royal, Princess Mary, daughter of King George V and Queen Mary. A previous plaque had been unveiled on the original house in 1912 by the Duke of Westminster, but this was lost when the house was demolished and rebuilt in the 1920s.

## 19 South Audley Street, W1K 2BN

Thomas Goode & Co, founded in 1827, is a retailer of luxury tableware, china, silverware and glassware. A ledger dated 1899 shows that Florence's household purchased glass dishes, vases, a teapot, jugs and a lemon squeezer.

*Ledger detailing purchases for Florence's household*

## 372 Strand, WC2R 0JJ

The former Exeter Hall once stood on the site of the Strand Palace Hotel. That was where the opera singer, Jenny Lind, who was known as the Swedish Nightingale, gave a concert in support of *The Nightingale Fund* which raised over £1,800. *See also* WHITEHALL.

## 1 Stratton St, W1J 8LA

Florence wrote from Scutari to her friend, Angela Burdett-Coutts, who lived here. Florence described how an inability to dry laundry gave rise to "the sodden misery in the hospital". Baroness Burdett-Coutts, of the Coutts banking family, one of the wealthiest women in the country, was a great philanthropist. When she received Florence's letter she consulted her friend, Charles Dickens, and found a practical solution. She ordered a drying machine that could be shipped out to Scutari in parts and reassembled on site. The dimensions were 6ft × 6ft × 7ft (1.8m × 1.8m × 2.1m). When the drying machine arrived, Florence wrote a grateful letter of thanks.

## Tyers Street, SE11 5HL

As a young girl of ten years old, Florence went on an evening visit to Vauxhall Pleasure Gardens with some of her Smith relatives. She was captivated by the illuminated castle with musicians inside, enjoyed the fireworks and the fountains, and the boy soldiers playing music. One of the highlights of the evening appears to have been travelling back by boat at 11 o'clock at night.

Part of the site was opened as a public park in the late 20th century.

## 20 Upper Berkeley Street, W1H 7PF

Elizabeth Garrett Anderson, the first woman to qualify as a doctor in England, lived here from 1865 to 1874. Whilst living here, she set up her medical practice. Florence and Garrett Anderson were contemporaries and knew each other, but did not always agree. Garrett Anderson trained as a nurse before training as a doctor. When asked why she did not wish to stay as a nurse, she replied that she would rather earn a thousand than twenty pounds a year. Florence thought women doctors were trying to be men, and only made third rate men. They also differed on the Contagious Diseases Act. It was Garrett Anderson's daughter, Louisa, a doctor like her mother, who certified Florence's death at her home in South Street in 1910. *See also* Houses of Parliament, North View.

*Florence's death certificate with Louisa Garrett Anderson's signature*

## 20 Upper Wimpole Street, W1G 6LZ

Ethel Gordon Fenwick, nursing reformer, campaigned for the professional development of nurses, especially the registration of nurses. Florence disagreed with registration based on examinations alone, fearing it would disadvantage working class women with little formal education. The Nurses Registration Act was passed in 1919. Mrs Fenwick became State Registered Nurse Number 1.

## Victoria Embankment Gardens, WC2R 2AB

A bronze statue of the 19th century philosopher, John Stuart Mill, by Thomas Woolner can be found in these gardens. Mill was introduced to Florence by the public health reformer Sir Edwin Chadwick, and they became friends and regular correspondents. He was an MP and campaigned for women's rights. There is a blue plaque to him at 40 Queen Anne's Gate, and a green plaque at 18 Kensington Square.

## Waterloo Place, SW1Y 4AR

The statue of Florence, sculpted by Arthur George Walker, was erected in 1915. Around the top of the plinth are four reliefs depicting scenes from Florence's life: Florence greeting wounded soldiers, Florence offering advice in a hospital, Florence meeting with senior army officers and Florence as an elderly lady surrounded by graduate

*Turkish lantern, or fanoos, used in Scutari in the Crimean War. It is thought to have been carried by Florence on her nightly rounds of the wards*

nurses. The statue of Florence herself is a familiar image and one that was popularised following the Crimean War. However, the lamp that Florence is seen holding is wrong. It is a Greek, or genie, lamp whereas Florence used a fanoos, or Turkish lamp, in the Crimean War. Both the Florence Nightingale Museum and the National Army Museum have the correct style of lamp in their collections.

Next to Florence stands a statue of Sidney Herbert, who was Secretary at War when Britain entered the Crimean War in 1854. Florence had met Sidney and his wife Elizabeth in Rome in the 1840s and became lifelong friends with the couple. It was Sidney who asked Florence to recruit and train nurses for the military hospital at Scutari. Following the Crimean War, he also worked alongside her on reforming health care in the army. The statue, by J H Foley, was originally erected outside the War Office in 1866 before being moved here in 1915.

Completing the trio of memorials is the Guards Crimean War Memorial, which commemorates the 2,152 men of the Brigade of Guards who died in the Crimean War. Sculpted by John Bell, it is made from the bronze of cannons captured at the siege of Sebastopol. Erected in 1861, the monument was moved slightly in 1914 to make space for the statues of Florence and Sidney Herbert.

## 57 Waterloo Road, SE1 8WA

The James Clerk Maxwell Building of King's College London is the modern-day home of the Florence Nightingale Faculty of Nursing, Midwifery and Palliative Care, which started life in 1860 as Florence's School of Nursing. Over the years the school has evolved, merging with the Olive Haydon School of Midwifery in 1991. The Faculty consists of four departments: Adult Nursing,

Child & Family Health, Mental Health Nursing and Midwifery, plus the Cicely Saunders Institute of Palliative Care, Policy and Rehabilitation, which was included in 2017. *See also* KING STREET, ST THOMAS STREET, ST THOMAS' HOSPITAL.

## Wellcome Collection, 183 Euston Road, NW1 2BE

Florence is sometimes thought of as a hypochondriac, feigning illness when it suited her. However, she was genuinely ill throughout much of her life, regularly suffering bouts of Crimean Fever, a bacterial infection picked up during the Crimean War. In 1995, David Young, a scientist at the Wellcome Institute, studied Florence's symptoms and records. He concluded that she suffered from chronic brucellosis, a bacterial infection contracted from infected animals, unpasteurised milk and raw meat. In later life, Florence also suffered from spondylitis, inflammation of bones in the spine, which meant she had to be carried to and from her bed.

The Wellcome Collection and Library has an archive of material relating to Florence.

## Westminster Abbey, 20 Deans Yard, SW1P 3PA

When Florence died in 1910, a funeral and burial in Westminster Abbey were offered to her family but they declined the offer as Florence had not wanted any fuss and had requested a quiet, private funeral. Instead, she was buried in the graveyard of St Margaret's Church near the family home of Embley Park in East Wellow, Hampshire.

Inside the Abbey is a Nurses' Memorial Chapel, designed by Sebastian Comper, which was created in 1950 to remember all nurses from the UK and Commonwealth who died in World War Two. The chapel was rededicated to Florence Nightingale on the centenary of her death in 2010. Every May the Abbey hosts the annual Florence Nightingale Commemoration Service, which celebrates nursing and midwifery.

American poet, Henry Wadsworth Longfellow, who was inspired by Florence to write the poem *Santa Filomena*, has a bust in Poets Corner. His poem popularised the phrase "The Lady with the Lamp", which the soldiers in the Crimean War had used to describe Florence.

### Whitehall, SW1A 2AY

Near to Horse Guards is an equestrian statue of Prince George, Duke of Cambridge. The duke was a soldier and served in the Crimean War at the battles of Alma, Balaclava and Inkerman, and at the Siege of Sebastopol. He was chairman of *The Nightingale Fund* when it was established in 1855 to raise funds for and recognise the work of Florence in the war. *See also* DARTMOUTH PARK HILL.

Inside the Banqueting House is the Royal United Services Institute, which holds extensive collections on military conflicts, including the Crimean War. Following her death, the executors of Florence's will gave her medals and the Nightingale Jewel to the Institute. These are now on display at the National Army Museum. *See also* ALBEMARLE STREET, NATIONAL ARMY MUSEUM.

### 89 Wimbledon Parkside, SW19 5LR

Sir Edwin Saunders, Queen Victoria's dentist and the first dentist to be knighted, was also Florence's dentist. In 1867 she wrote to him: "I have broken four of my teeth lately (probably with gnashing my teeth at ministers!!)... I doubt whether even your skill can do anything for me."

## 85 York Road, Lambeth, SE1 7NJ

The General Lying-In Hospital, formerly on this site, was one of the first maternity hospitals in the country. They provided care for married women, and would also treat unmarried women if it was their first pregnancy. The building is a short walk from St Thomas' Hospital. Florence praised the quality of their care when her probationers received midwifery training there. "Lying-in" was a Victorian term for childbirth and the bed-rest that was prescribed afterwards. In 1871 Florence published *Introductory notes on lying-in institutions : together with a proposal for organising an institution for training midwives and midwifery nurses*. The building is now part of the Premier Inn Hotel Waterloo.

## Zoological Society of London, Regent's Park, NW1 4RY

London Zoo was founded in 1826, to form a collection of animals and study them. It opened in Regent's Park on 27 April 1828 and Florence visited a few weeks later. The 8-year-old Florence wrote to her paternal grandmother in early July 1828 describing what she had seen: "two leopards, two bears, two parrots, two emus (which are very large birds), two rabbits, one lion, two cockatoos".

# SUGGESTED WALKS

Although you may be inspired to visit all the locations mentioned in this book, here are a few clusters of locations relating to Florence Nightingale within walking distance of each other. When visiting these areas and locations, please refer to the A to Z chapter for information about each location.

# MAYFAIR

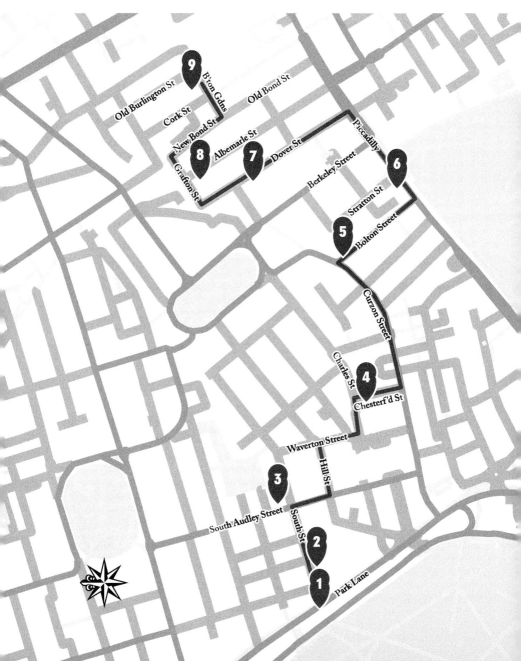

Start at the corner of Park Lane and South Street at Aldford House, the official address is Park Street **(1)**, with the green plaque to actress Anna Neagle. Go down South Street and stop outside Number 10 **(2)** to view the blue plaque commemorating Florence. Continue down South Street to the corner of South Audley Street **(3)** for Thomas Goode & Co. Turn right into South Audley Street, then left into Hill Street and right into Waverton Street. Follow Waverton Street to the end, where it turns left and becomes Charles Street. Then turn right into Chesterfield Street and stop at Number 9 **(4)**. Turn left into Curzon Street, then right into Bolton Street **(5)**. Continue to the end of Bolton Street, turn left into Piccadilly and stop at the corner of Piccadilly and Stratton Street for Number 1 **(6)**. Carry on along Piccadilly, cross Berkeley Street and turn left into Dover Street, stopping at Number 31 **(7)**. Carry on along Dover Street and continue straight on where it becomes Grafton Street and follow it round to the right. Stop on the corner of Albemarle Street **(8)** for the House of Garrard. Cross Albemarle Street, turn right into New Bond Street and then left into Burlington Gardens. On the left, located between Cork Street **(9)** and Old Burlington Street, was the site of the Burlington Hotel.

# ST JAMES'S

1 Piccadilly

Duke St

2 Jermyn Street

Duke of York St

4

5 St James's Sq

3

12

6 King St

St James's Square

9

11 Pall Mall

8 Carlton Gdns

Waterloo Pl

7 St James's Street

Pall Mall

10 Carlton House Ter

The walk starts on Piccadilly at Fortnum & Mason **(1)**. Turn down Duke Street, to the right-hand side of Fortnum & Mason, then left into Jermyn Street to perfumier Floris **(2)**. Turn right into Duke of York Street and then right into St James's Square **(3)**. Continue round the square to Number 12 **(4)** and the London Library at Number 14 **(5)**. Turn right into King Street and stop at Number 26 **(6)**. Go straight on to the end of King Street, turn left into St James's Street, then left again into Pall Mall. Stop at Number 59 **(7)**. Cross to the other side of Pall Mall to the Royal Automobile Club at Number 89 **(8)**. Continue along Pall Mall to the Reform Club at Number 104 **(9)**. Turn into Carlton Gardens, to the right of the Reform Club, then left into Carlton House Terrace and stop at Number 4 **(10)**. Continue along Carlton House Terrace and turn left onto Waterloo Place. On the left-hand side is the Athenaeum at Number 107 Pall Mall **(11)**. On the other side of Pall Mall at the junction with Waterloo Place **(12)** is a trio of memorials relating to the Crimean War.

# WESTMINSTER

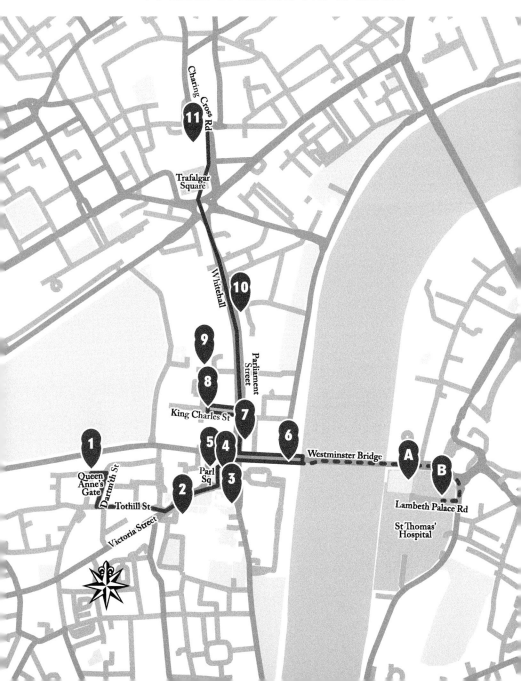

Charing Cross Rd

**11**

Trafalgar
Square

Whitehall

**10**

**9**

Parliament
Street

**8**

King Charles St  **7**

**6**  Westminster Bridge  **A**

**B**

**1**

**5**  **4**

Queen
Anne's
Gate  Dartmth St

Parl
Sq  **3**

**2**

Tothill St

Lambeth Palace Rd

St Thomas'
Hospital

Victoria Street

Start in Queen Anne's Gate at Number 16 **(1)**. At the end of the street turn right into Dartmouth Street, then left into Tothill Street. Turn right at the end of the street and cross over Victoria Street at the traffic lights and turn left to Westminster Abbey **(2)**. Walk round to the left side of Westminster Abbey to St Margaret's Church **(3)**. Cross into the middle of Parliament Square **(4)** to view the statues of Mahatma Gandhi, Benjamin Disraeli, Lord Beaconsfield, and Viscount Palmerston. Head towards the edge of the green opposite Big Ben, where you'll get a good view of the Houses of Parliament **(5)**. Cross at the traffic lights towards Big Ben and go straight on into Bridge Street on the left side of Big Ben. Walk a short way onto Westminster Bridge to get a view across the river Thames of St Thomas' Hospital **(6)**. *[Optional diversion – cross the bridge to the hospital to see the statue of Mary Seacole* **(A)** *and to visit the Florence Nightingale Museum* **(B)***]*. Return down Bridge Street. Turn right at the traffic lights from the corner of Parliament Square into Parliament Street and stop at Number 5 **(7)**. Cross over to the other side of the street and turn left into King Charles Street **(8)**. Retrace your steps back up King Charles Street and turn left into Whitehall. On the left is Number 10 Downing Street **(9)**. Keep walking along Whitehall **(10)** for the Banqueting House across the road and equestrian statue of Prince George, Duke of Cambridge, which sits in the middle of the road. Carry on up Whitehall to Trafalgar Square, cross straight onto the square using the traffic light crossings and, staying on the right-hand side, go into Charing Cross Road, with St Martin-in-the-Fields Church on the opposite side of the road to your right. Behind the National Gallery, on your left, is the National Portrait Gallery **(11)**.

# CITY OF LONDON

5

6

Cornhill

Lombard St

4

Princes
St

3

Poultry

Gresham St

Cheapside

2

St M's Le Grand

7

New
Change

1

King Ed St

8

St Paul's
Churchyard

St Bart's
Hospital

Queen Victoria St

9

10

New Bridge
St

11

Fleet St

12

Start this walk at St Bartholomew's Hospital **(1)** in West Smith-
field. Facing the main entrance, go down the left side of the hospital
into Little Britain. Cross King Edward Street at the traffic lights
and turn right, then left into Postman's Park and go through it to St
Martin's le Grand. Cross at the traffic lights and turn right to the
Lord Raglan Pub **(2)**. Turn left into Gresham Street to the Guildhall **(3)**. Return to Gresham Street, carry on to the junction and
turn right into Princes Street, crossing over onto the left-hand side
of the street. Then turn left for the Bank of England **(4)**. Cross
Threadneedle Street at the traffic lights and turn left down the side
of the Royal Exchange into Cornhill for Number 65 **(5)**. Retrace
your steps slightly and turn left into Birchin Lane stopping at
Number 20 **(6)**. Turn right into Lombard Street back to Bank Junction and cross via the traffic lights into Poultry. Continue into
Cheapside and, at the far end, cross New Change at the traffic lights
to St Paul's Cathedral **(7)**. Walk to the front of the Cathedral, facing
the main entrance, go down the right side of the cathedral. Cross
over to the other side of St Paul's Churchyard at the double set of
traffic lights. Go straight ahead down Sermon Lane and Peter's Hill
towards the river Thames. At the bottom, turn right into Queen
Victoria Street by the College of Arms **(8)**. Carry on along Queen
Victoria Street to Number 160 **(9)**. Keep straight on and turn right
at The Blackfriar Pub into New Bridge Street. At Ludgate Circus,
turn left into Fleet Street to Number 85 **(10)**. Carry on along Fleet
Street to Number 169 **(11)** and then further on to the Royal Courts
of Justice **(12)**.

# BLOOMSBURY

Start at the British Library **(1)** on Euston Road. Facing the library, turn left to Euston Station **(2)**. Then cross to the other side of Euston Road for the Wellcome Collection **(3)** at Number 183. Facing the Wellcome, turn left and then right into Gordon Street. Continue straight on into Gordon Square and stop at Number 14 **(4)**. Turn right out of the square into Byng Place and on into Torrington Place, cross Malet Street and turn left into Gower Street and stop at Number 47 **(5)**. Carry on along Gower Street, past Bedford Square and keep going straight on into Bloomsbury Street. Turn left into Great Russell Street and go past the British Museum. Carry on into Bloomsbury Square **(6)** to Number 23 at the corner with Bedford Place. Carry on past the square into Bloomsbury Place and cross Southampton Row. Turn left and walk past the parade of shops, then turn right into Cosmo Place. Turn left into Queen Square **(7)** and stop at Number 12. Cross the gardens in the middle of the square and turn right then left to exit the gardens and the square into Great Ormond Street. Continue past the children's hospital, cross over Lamb's Conduit Street and turn left into Millman Street. At the far end, turn right into Guilford Street and right again into Doughty Street. Number 48-49 is the Charles Dickens Museum **(8)**.

# FLORENCE NIGHTINGALE MUSEUM

As the bicentenary of the birth of Florence Nightingale approached, 2020 was to be marked by the World Health Organisation as "International Year of the Nurse and Midwife" in her honour. Our team at the Florence Nightingale Museum appreciated that this was a fantastic opportunity not only to celebrate her life and achievements, but also stress her ongoing relevance to all our lives today. We had been preparing for this special anniversary for over three years, but little did we know that nature would serve us the most dramatic stage on which to present her story, in the form of a worldwide pandemic. The principles of compassionate and skilled healthcare and statistical data analysis which Nightingale pioneered and promoted throughout her career, would be at the forefront of the global response.

With the museum forced to close and the cancellation of numerous global events we had helped to plan and co-ordinate, our celebrations were understandably somewhat muted. Instead, the museum and its stories of the founder of modern nursing, which we are proud to share, played a crucial role in inspiring our healthcare workers.

The Florence Nightingale Museum, an independent charity (registered charity number: 299576), is based at St Thomas' Hospital, Lambeth, on the site of Nightingale's first purpose-built nursing school. The collection contains about 3,000 objects including many of her letters, books and personal items. A high percentage of these were collected by Dame Alicia Lloyd Still, a former matron of St Thomas', who gathered the items for the purpose of education and remembering the accomplishments of her inspiration.

Popular exhibits include: a "fanoos lantern" believed to belong to "the Lady with the Lamp", which she used during her nightly walks at Scutari Hospital during the Crimean War; her medicine chest

*Florence with Athena, the owlet she rescued in Athens, drawn by her sister Parthenope*

which journeyed with her from the UK to the famous conflict that saw Nightingale catapulted to fame; and "Athena" her beloved pet owl, who sadly passed away under mysterious circumstances whilst Nightingale was preparing to do her duty caring for our nation's soldiers. Exhibits are presented in colourful and theatrical displays. These surprise many visitors, who frequently describe the museum as one of the capital's "small gems" and a "must see" for anyone with an interest in Victorian Britain, the history of healthcare, or iconic women. Nightingale's story is frequently brought to life with the use of character performers, who provide a warm welcome and a highly engaging way of learning, as well as one of London's most popular selfies!

The museum's permanent displays tell tales of Nightingale's life in chronological order and are supported by a temporary exhibition area. At the time of writing, the temporary exhibition had been installed to celebrate Nightingale's bicentenary.

*Nightingale in 200 Objects, People and Places* was co-curated with the nursing community and various heritage attractions with a shared interest in her life. The exhibition not only shines a light on some of the lesser known and more quirky aspects of Nightingale's life, but also considers her legacy, celebrating the successes of some of those who have followed in her footsteps.

The museum also contains a dedicated *Family Corner*, which was created in conjunction with the "Nightingale Academy" from St Thomas' Hospital - those nurses who have achieved the highest levels of patient care. In this area families can explore the journey into nursing of both Nightingale and these contemporary figures, recognising the different career paths taken and considerable opportunities available. Whilst children have great fun dressing up in historic and contemporary nursing uniforms and exploring a quiz trail, it is hoped some will recognise the sense of fulfilment a career in nursing can offer, hopefully taking up the mantle in the future. Will the museum one day inspire the next Nightingale?

Over the past 4 years the museum has developed considerably and gone from strength to strength, winning several industry awards and attracting increasing numbers of domestic and international tourists. The museum also operates widely respected services within and for the local community, including a hugely popular schools programme, a variety of talks and tours and diverse volunteering opportunities. In the future, the museum plans to become "The Florence Nightingale Museum of Nursing", a venue celebrating and thanking all who nurse.

More information about the museum can be found on their website at **www.florence-nightingale.co.uk**. Do explore it to find out how to visit, see what's happening, learn more about Florence's life and visit the online shop.

**David Green, Director, Florence Nightingale Museum**

# FLORENCE
## IN THE
# UNITED
# KINGDOM

Florence travelled quite extensively in the United Kingdom. Her family's homes were in Derbyshire and Hampshire, and she had friends and family in many different parts of the country. She travelled for pleasure, for leisure and to follow her interests.

## Buckinghamshire

CLAYDON HOUSE has been the ancestral home of the Verney family since 1620. Sir Harry Verney MP was Florence's brother-in-law, having married her sister Parthenope in 1858. He was a great supporter of Florence's work on health reforms and was often referred to in Parliament as "the Member for Miss Nightingale". Florence was a frequent visitor to Claydon, particularly during the summer months, and had her own set of rooms in the house. A portrait of Florence by the artist W B Richmond, which was commissioned by the Verneys, hangs in what was once her bedroom.

*Parthenope Lady Verney, Florence and Sir Harry Verney at Claydon House, c.1880*

Although Sir Harry and Parthenope did not have any children together, Florence was a favourite "aunt" to Sir Harry's grandchildren from his first marriage. She was also godmother to three of the Verney girls; Ruth, daughter of Sir Harry's eldest son Edmund, and Kathleen and Gwendolen, daughters of his youngest son Frederick.

In the 1880s, an annual highlight was a day trip to Claydon by the Nightingale probationers from St Thomas' Hospital, during which a chosen few were granted an audience with Florence herself.

Today, Claydon House is in the care of the National Trust and is open to the public. Surrounding the house is the CLAYDON ESTATE, which is still in the hands of the Verney family. In the Courtyard is the carriage that Florence used during her time in the Crimean War. *See* HARRODS in the A TO Z.

## Derbyshire

Florence's father, William Edward Shore, inherited the estate of LEA HURST near Matlock from his great uncle Peter Nightingale, whose family had made their money in lead mining. As required by Peter Nightingale's will, William changed his surname to

*Lithograph from a drawing by Parthenope Nightingale of the exterior of Lea Hurst, near Matlock, Derbyshire*

Nightingale in 1815. The family spent summer months in Derbyshire.

The estate passed out of the Nightingale family after World War Two. Today Lea Hurst is a private residence, with some rooms occasionally available for booking.

There are many connections with the Nightingale family in the nearby villages of LEA and HOLLOWAY, including a school, a former reading room and a chapel.

Florence's great aunt Elizabeth Evans (Aunt Evans), lived nearby in CROMFORD BRIDGE HOUSE, where Florence nursed her. After Aunt Evans died in 1852, Florence's mother suggested using the house as a private nursing home for Florence to run. But Florence had other ideas.

## Hampshire

Florence's parents bought EMBLEY PARK in 1825 as their main residence, spending their winters in the south and the summer months at their other home in Derbyshire. When Florence was aged 16, she experienced her "call to service" whilst sitting under one of the large cedar trees on the estate. The house today is a privately owned boarding school and is not open to the public.

*Lithograph from a drawing by Parthenope Nightingale of Embley Park near Romsey, Hampshire c. August 1856.*

Florence was often seen in the local village of WELLOW and was well known to the villagers. WELLOW PRIMARY SCHOOL was founded in 1828 by Florence's father in a cottage provided by him at WARNERS FARM.

The parish church of ST MARGARET OF ANTIOCH is where Florence was laid to rest upon her death in 1910. Her funeral took place on 20th August and, in accordance with her wishes, her tombstone is very plain. The church has some memorabilia relating to Florence and, every May, a commemoration service is held there to remember Florence.

*The Nightingale family grave in the churchyard of St Margaret, Wellow*

BROADLANDS was the Hampshire estate of Lord Palmerston and his wife Emily Lamb. It was at a dinner party thrown by the Palmerstons that Florence first met her long-time suitor, Richard Monckton Milnes.

## Kent

Following her return from the Crimean War, Florence visited the sick and wounded soldiers at the hospital at FORT PITT in CHATHAM. Her work with the *Royal Commission on the Sanitary Condition of the Army* led to Florence selecting Fort Pitt for the new ARMY MEDICAL SCHOOL. This opened in 1861, but moved to Netley in Hampshire two years later, a move that Florence opposed.

Exhausted by work and grieving for her mother, Fanny, who had passed away in February 1880, Florence spent three weeks at THE GRANVILLE HOTEL in RAMSGATE. Located on the seafront, the hotel was a luxurious place to stay. Today it has been remodelled into apartments.

## Liverpool

Florence was heavily associated with nursing in Liverpool and had two papers presented at a meeting of the National Association for the Promotion of Social Science there in 1858.

Following that meeting, local philanthropist, William Rathbone VI, liaised with Florence to create the first professional District Nursing service in 1859. This provided care for the sick in their own homes in Liverpool. Today his district nursing service is the QUEEN'S NURSING INSTITUTE.

In 1862, Rathbone, with guidance from Florence, established a School of Nursing at LIVERPOOL ROYAL INFIRMARY. Nurses from this training school would go on to work both at the Royal Infirmary and in the district nursing service. Florence and Rathbone remained friends and corresponded regularly throughout their lifetimes.

The Royal Infirmary on BROWNLOW HILL was redesigned in the 1880s by Liverpool architect, Sir Alfred Waterhouse who corresponded with Florence on the design and incorporated her favoured "pavilion" design into his plans.

Florence sent 12 nurses and 18 probationers from the School of Nursing at St Thomas' Hospital, London to the LIVERPOOL WORK-HOUSE INFIRMARY in 1865. Paid for by William Rathbone VI, the team of nurses was led by Agnes Jones who was held in high regard by Florence. Sadly, Jones died of typhus at the age of 35. Florence commented "I looked upon hers as one of the most valuable lives in England". Florence firmly believed in the benefits of trained nurses providing healthcare in the workhouses and her actions led to many other workhouses improving their healthcare.

## Northern Ireland

Florence travelled to BELFAST in summer 1852 with family friends, Dr and Mrs Fowler of Salisbury, to attend the annual meeting of the British Association for the Advancement of Science, at the MAY STREET CHURCH. The organisation, now known as the British Science Association, aims to aid the promotion and development of science.

## Oxford

Florence had a 30-year friendship with Benjamin Jowett, Church of England priest, Professor of Greek and Master of BALL-IOL COLLEGE. Like Florence, he advocated the use of statistics in medicine. They corresponded regularly and Jowett often visited Florence in London, administering Holy Communion to her. Florence also occasionally went to Oxford. It has been suggested that Jowett was in love with Florence and proposed marriage to her, but to date no evidence has been found to support this.

Florence visited Oxford with her father in 1847 to attend

meetings of the British Association for the Advancement of Science, now known as the British Science Association, where she heard astronomer Sir John Herschel discuss the discovery of Neptune. On visits to Oxford, Florence enjoyed tea at CHRIST CHURCH and attended services at MAGDALENE COLLEGE and NEW COLLEGE.

Florence also corresponded with Sir Henry Dyke Acland, physician and Regius Professor of Medicine at Oxford. Acland was physician to the RADCLIFFE INFIRMARY, which received their first trained matron, Flora Masson, courtesy of Florence in 1891. Acland was also curator of the BODLEIAN LIBRARY, which holds an archive of material relating to Florence.

## Scotland

Whilst on a trip to Ireland in 1852, Florence was called urgently to BIRK HALL in ABERDEENSHIRE where her sister Parthenope had been taken ill. Florence arrived in mid-September accompanied by her maid, Mariette. Parthenope had been visiting the home of Sir James Clark, Queen Victoria's physician. Once her sister was well enough, Florence accompanied her home to Lea Hurst.

Florence stayed at Birk Hall again, in September 1856, when she was invited by Queen Victoria to visit BALMORAL CASTLE. The Queen wanted to hear personally about her work in the Crimean War and her ideas for health reform in the British Army. Florence travelled to Scotland with her father and spent a few days in EDINBURGH on the way. As well as meeting with the Queen, Florence attended a number of balls at Court and attended church with the royal family. She also entertained the Queen to tea at Birk Hall. The ultimate result of this visit was the setting up of a Royal Commission to look into the state of healthcare in the Army.

In 1872, Florence sent a group of trained "Nightingale Nurses" from St Thomas' Hospital, London to THE ROYAL INFIRMARY OF EDINBURGH at the request of its new Medical Superintendent, Deputy Surgeon-General Charles Hamilton Fasson. The group of 17 nurses included Angelique Lucille Pringle, a Scot. She was a particular favourite of Florence and was nicknamed "The Pearl". As matron, Pringle overhauled the training of nurses at the Infirmary and it effectively became a second Nightingale School of Nursing. Florence referred to the Royal Infirmary as "the best hospital" in the United Kingdom.

## Surrey

WAVERLEY, near Farnham, was the country home of Florence's relatives, the Nicholsons. Florence was a frequent visitor. In early 1842, the cousins put on an amateur theatrical production of Shakespeare's "The Merchant of Venice". Florence's sister, Parthenope, painted the scenery; Florence's cousins acted in the production; and Florence was the stage manager.

The house is now known as WAVERLEY ABBEY HOUSE, and is available for hire as a corporate venue. One of the meeting rooms is named the Florence Room. It is named for the former Waverley Abbey, built in the 12th Century. The ruins of the abbey are managed by English Heritage.

## Warwickshire

The country home of Florence's great friends, the Bracebridges, was Atherstone Hall in the market town of ATHERSTONE. Florence stayed with them several times. The Hall was demolished, but the Dower House remains, and is now a restaurant, called Chapel House.

## Wiltshire

Wilton House, near Salisbury, is the family home of the Earl and Countess of Pembroke. It was also the country residence of Sidney Herbert, younger son of the 11th Earl of Pembroke. Sidney Herbert, born 1810, and his wife, Elizabeth, were friends of Florence, and she stayed with them at Wilton House. Sidney Herbert died in 1861 at the age of 50, and is buried in the churchyard at Wilton.

The estate is an English Heritage property open to the public during the summer.

## Worcestershire

During the 19th Century, Malvern was a popular place for water cures – using mineral water for medicinal purposes. Florence travelled there many times, between 1848 and 1868, staying for several weeks at a time.

## Yorkshire

Lotherton Hall, near Aberford, West Yorkshire is the former home of the Gascoigne family. Gwendolen Gascoigne, one of Florence's godchildren, was the daughter of Sir Douglas Galton and Florence's cousin Marianne (nee Nicholson). The hall is one of the sites of the Leeds Museums and Galleries. In 2020/21 it held an online exhibition celebrating the Bicentenary of Florence Nightingale, displaying letters and objects connected with Florence.

The Leeds General Infirmary, founded in 1771, moved to a new site in Great George Street in 1869. The architect of the new hospital, Sir George Gilbert Scott, was influenced by Florence's ideas on pavilion wards, and incorporated them into the building.

# FLORENCE
## IN THE
# CRIMEAN WAR

The Crimean War broke out in October 1853 between the Ottoman Empire (Turkey) and Imperialist Russia. The following year, Britain and France formed an alliance with Turkey and entered the war, as they feared Russian expansion would threaten their own territories. Both Britain and France were also keen to limit Russian naval power in the Black Sea. In 1855, the Kingdom of Sardinia also entered the war alongside Turkey, Britain and France.

There were three main battles during the war: Alma on 20 September, Balaclava on 25 October and Inkerman on 5 November 1854. In addition, the Siege of Sebastapol lasted from October 1854 to September 1855. For the British, the most famous single part of the conflict was the disastrous Charge of the Light Brigade, which became immortalised in a poem by Alfred, Lord Tennyson.

It was news of the high level of casualties at the battle of the Alma that prompted Florence to go out to the Crimean War.

## Recruitment

When Secretary at War, Sidney Herbert, asked Florence to assist with the war effort and recruit and train nurses to go out to the Crimean War she tackled the task with her usual gusto. Hundreds of women applied to go out "to the East", so Florence employed a rigorous selection process to try and ensure she got nurses of the required calibre.

A number of ladies helped Florence with her selection process, including her sister, Parthenope, her friends, Selina Bracebridge and Liz Herbert, and a friend with nursing experience, Mary Stanley. Over the course of the war, 229 women went out to the East to be nurses in the military hospitals. Florence and 38 nurses in the initial party paved the way for those that followed.

## Travel to Scutari

Florence and her party of 38 nurses did not all set off together. The sisters from the Convent of Mercy, Parker's Row, Bermondsey, had set off first, on 17 October 1854, and had been instructed to wait for the rest of the party in Paris.

On Saturday 21 October 1854, Florence set off from her parents' rented accommodation on Cavendish Square and stopped off at Belgrave Square, the home of the Herberts, where Sidney Herbert gave a rousing speech to the party. She travelled from London Bridge by train to the Kent coast, and then boarded a cross channel steamer to take her to France. From there, she made her way to Paris.

On 23 October 1854, Florence's friends, the Bracebridges, and other members of the party left London Bridge and travelled via Boulogne, where they were warmly welcomed at the Hotel des Bains. The whole party was reunited later that day in Paris. The next day, the party set off to Lyons by train. The railway line through France had not been completed, so on 25 October they continued their journey by boat down the river Rhone to Valence, where they again joined the train and travelled to Marseilles, arriving in the evening.

On Friday 27 October, the party boarded the P&O mail steamer *Vectis* and left Marseilles. The voyage was rough and many of the party suffered from sea sickness. On the way they passed within sight of Sicily, before landing in Malta on 30 October. The journey continued and they arrived in Constantinople (modern day Istanbul) on Saturday 4 November 1854. From there they made their way to the Barrack Hospital in Scutari, known today as Üsküdar.

Upon arrival, casualties from the battle of Inkerman were streaming into Scutari Barrack Hospital and it was the wounded

from this battle that were the first to be tended to by Florence and
her nurses.

## Florence's 38

Of the 38 women who volunteered to go to Scutari with Florence, one of those was her housekeeper, Mrs Clarke, who was inva-
lided home in April 1855. Then there were the nuns and women
from the religious orders of Bermondsey Convent, Norwood
House, St John's House and Miss Sellon's Sisters of Mercy. Plus,
there were women with nursing experience. Florence insisted that
all the nurses sent to Scutari should be subject to her authority,

*Register of Nurses detailing the 229 women who served as nurses at the British
military hospitals during the Crimean War. The first name listed is Florence's*

rather than that of the military medical staff, or their own religious superiors. All of the 38 agreed to this.

The Roman Catholic Bermondsey Convent sent five nuns, including the Reverend Mother Mary Clare (Georgiana Moore). The others were Sister Mary Gonzaga (Georgiana Bonie Barrie), Sister de Chantal (Maria Huddon), Sister Stanislaus (Margaret Jones) and Sister Anastasia (Sarah Kelly). The Reverend Mother and Sister Mary Gonzaga returned home early, but the other three remained until the end of the war and, in due course, would be awarded the Royal Red Cross for their efforts.

Another five Roman Catholic nuns went to the Crimea from the Convent of Our Lady of the Orphans, also known as Our Lady of Fidelity and as Norwood House. All five of them, Justine Chabrillac, Marie Therese McClean, Eliza Keith Forbes, Elinor O'Dwyer and Frances Jane Purnell, were sent home as "incompetent" or "unfit" in December 1854.

The religious community of St John's House, which was a training institution for nurses in hospitals, sent six sisters. Four of them, M A Bournelt, M A Coyle, Emma Fagg and Ann Higgins, were also sent home as "incompetent" in January 1855. Of the other two, Rebecca Lawfield was also sent home and Elizabeth Drake sadly died at Balaclava in August 1855.

There were eight Church of England nuns from the Society of the Sisters of Mercy of Devonport, more commonly known as Sellonites after their founder Priscilla Lydia Sellon. The Sellonite sisters Harriet Erskine, Sarah Terrot and Emma Langston returned home sick in April 1855. Clara Sharp and Etheldreda Pillars returned home in ill health in December that year, and Elizabeth Wheeler went home sick as soon as she arrived. Only Elizabeth

Turnbull and Margaret Goodman stayed in the Crimea until the end of the war, returning home in July 1856.

The remainder of the nurses came from various hospitals or were women with medical experience. A few of these were dismissed for intoxication and sent home, including A Faulkner, S Jones and Margaret Williams. Others, such as C Blake, Elizabeth Smith and M Williams returned home through illness, with Mrs Wilson being sent home immediately as she arrived ill.

One, E Grundy, returned home at her own request in November 1855 but a few lasted the course and returned home at the end of the war, sometimes accompanying detachments of soldiers home, including S Davy, E Hawkins and Mrs Parker. Mrs Roberts also stayed until the end, returning home with Florence in August 1856.

In addition to Sister Elizabeth Drake, another of the original 38 nurses died during the Crimean War when S Barnes sadly died of fever in April 1855.

## Medical Care

Casualties on all sides were high during the war, with more than 200,000 soldiers killed on the allied side and many thousands more wounded. Losses on the Russian side were much higher, estimated at over 500,000. The hospitals were overrun with casualties and, initially at least, ill-equipped to handle the numbers of wounded. Diseases such as cholera, typhoid and dysentery added huge numbers to those needing hospitalisation. More soldiers would die of disease during the war than of their battle wounds.

Upon arrival at the hospital, Florence was received by the hospital's Chief Medical Officer, Dr Duncan Menzies. Initially, the medical officers did not want Florence and her team of nurses interfering in the care of the soldiers, so they were put to work cleaning. Conditions in the hospital were horrific. There were not enough beds for the wounded and men were lying on the floor. There was filth everywhere, rats ran round and the smell was overpowering. Eventually, the number of casualties became so overwhelming that the doctors and medical officers relented and Florence and her nurses started caring for the soldiers.

Scutari Barrack Hospital was Florence's main base for the duration of her time in the Crimean War and it was here that she saw first-hand the true horror of the conditions for the sick and wounded.

Although the most famous of the hospitals used in the Crimean War, Scutari Barrack Hospital was not the only one. Others in Turkey included Scutari General Hospital, where the matron was Sarah Tebbut, and the Palace Hospital at Haidar Pasha, which was not under Florence's direct control. There was also the Stable Hospital and two hospital ships, a Turkish hulk and the British ship *Bombay*. The British also used Koulali Hospital, based in a cavalry barracks a few miles from Scutari, which was used by Sardinian troops later on in the war.

In addition, Smyrna Hospital was located in the Turkish barracks in the ancient Greek city of Smyrna, which is today known as Izmir, and a naval hospital was based at Therapia, known as Tarabya today. This was located in a suburb of Constantinople on the shores of the Bosphorus strait and was run by Mrs Eliza MacKenzie.

There were also two civilian hospitals in Turkey that were used by British troops. One was Abydos, near Gallipoli. The other was Renkioi located on the banks of the Dardanelles and close to Scutari. Designed by engineer, Isambard Kingdom Brunel, this was a prefabricated temporary hospital that was shipped out from

England. It was specifically designed to provide a sanitised and hygienic solution to the problem of patients contracting diseases such as malaria, cholera and dysentery. Florence referred to Renkioi Hospital as "those magnificent huts".

Across the Black Sea, in the Crimean war zone, there were two hospitals at Balaclava; the General Hospital and the Castle Hospital, which was on the Genoese Heights above Balaclava and was managed by Jane Shaw Stewart. Then there was the Monastery Hospital and a small camp hospital. There was another hospital in the port and seaside resort of Varna, in modern day Bulgaria, on the Black Sea, which was the main naval base for the British and French.

## Florence's Work

Florence became a household name because of her work tending the sick and wounded in the Crimean War.

Florence worked tirelessly overseeing every detail of the care of the soldiers, hardly resting and working herself to the point of exhaustion. In May 1855, she toured the military hospitals at Balaclava. She also visited the trenches at Sebastopol, where she was warmly greeted by the soldiers who cheered her arrival. While in the Crimea, Florence became very ill, collapsing with exhaustion and fever. Crimean Fever, as it became known, left her close to death and she was nursed back to health at the Castle Hospital. Florence then spent time during the summer of 1855 convalescing at the ambassador's residence in Therapia. While there, she received gifts from home: her sister, Parthenope, had made her a book called *Life and death of Athena, an owlet from the Parthenon*, and Sidney Herbert sent her a dog, a terrier.

However, she wasn't the only nurse to become famous as a result.

The British-Jamaican nurse Mary Seacole used her own resources to go out to the Crimea. She set up the "British Hotel" in the war zone near Balaclava, where she offered refreshments for sale and also nursed the wounded.

## Media Interest

The use of the telegraph, war correspondents such as William Howard Russell who reported for *The Times*, and war photography, pioneered by Roger Fenton, all contributed to families at home in Britain being fully aware of the horrors the war inflicted on the troops.

Fenton's photographs were published in the *Illustrated London News*. Fenton purposely avoided taking photographs of any dead or wounded soldiers but did photograph soldiers and military personnel, as well as the battle zones. However, there is no record of him photographing Florence, who famously disliked having her image taken.

Alongside the war reports featured in the newspapers of the day, there were also reports about the work of Florence and her nurses. It was this media coverage that made Florence a household name, particularly with letters sent home by the soldiers being published in the newspapers.

## The War is Over

The beginning of the end of the war came when the Russians evacuated Sebastopol in September 1855 and began the move towards peace talks. Although still officially at war, the main conflict was over. The Russian tsar, Alexander II, had no appetite to continue the war. France, which had sent more soldiers to the war and suffered more casualties than Britain, also started to push for peace.

On 30 March 1856, The Treaty of Paris was signed between the Russian Empire and the allied nations of the Ottoman Empire, the United Kingdom, France and the Kingdom of Sardinia. The Crimean War was finally over.

## Florence Travels Home

Although the Crimean War ended in March 1856, Florence did not leave immediately. She travelled home with her aunt, Mary Smith, known as Aunt Mai. Florence did not want to attract any attention to herself, so she travelled as Miss Smith. She journeyed home via Paris and London. She caught the train to the Derbyshire station at Whatstandwell, and walked from there to her home at Lea Hurst. She arrived home in August 1856.

## Aftermath and Fame

The Crimean War saw the instigation of Britain's highest medal of honour for the military, the Victoria Cross. Designed and made by London silversmith Hancocks, the idea for a medal to honour soldiers who went above and beyond the call of duty was first presented to Parliament in 1854. Both Queen Victoria and her husband, Prince Albert, supported the idea and in 1856 the final design was approved by the Queen. 111 men who served in the Crimean War were awarded the Victoria Cross for valour in the presence of the enemy.

Hancocks cast the original medals and continue to do so today. All Victoria Crosses are made from bronze supplied by the Central Ordnance Depot in Donnington, which is cut from cannons captured from the Russians at Sebastopol during the Crimean War. The medal takes the form of a Maltese Cross with a Royal Crown surmounted by a lion and the motto "For Valour". Each medal is inscribed on the reverse with the individual details of each recipient.

Such was the publicity surrounding the Crimean War, and the wave of national fervour it generated at the time, that names synonymous with the war became popular.

In London there are numerous roads named for the main battles of Alma, Balaclava and Inkerman, plus a Sebastopol, Scutari and Therapia Road. The battle of Alma also gave rise to *Alma* being used as a girl's name. Florence's popularity and fame with the British public led not only to a surge in the name *Florence* for baby girls, but to a host of streets and roads named in her honour. In London there are numerous Florence roads and streets, plus a Florence Gardens and a Florence Terrace. There are also various Nightingale roads and streets.

# FLORENCE NIGHTINGALE'S LEGACY

Florence Nightingale's work and legacy is so great that she is known throughout the world with many statues, memorials and organisations dedicated to her memory.

Florence left thousands of letters, many of which are available to the public, through archives and online. She published several books – the most famous of which is *Notes on Nursing: What it is and what it is not*. There are also a number of biographies about Florence.

Plays and films have been made of her life. The most famous being *The Lady with a Lamp* in 1951, which starred Anna Neagle in the title role. There are paintings which feature Florence and her image has appeared on the £10 banknote.

"Nightingale" nurses and midwives are able to join the alumni association, the Nightingale Fellowship, and International Nurses Day is celebrated on 12 May, Florence's birthday.

The Lady with the Lamp is remembered in many places both in the UK and across the world, as detailed below. However, the authors would be happy to hear of any other places where Florence is commemorated.

## Other London places

Statuettes of Florence can be found in the Guildhall Art Gallery, Two Temple Place and St John's Gate. There are stained-glass windows featuring Florence in St Olave Church in Hart Street and The Champion Pub in Wells Street. The frieze on the London School of Hygiene & Tropical Medicine in Gower Street includes Florence's name and the Science Museum has a number of objects in its collection belonging to Florence.

Established in 1929 as a living memorial to Florence, the Florence Nightingale Foundation develops leadership programmes for nurses and midwives and provides scholarships to extend their knowledge and skills. The idea for a foundation was originally announced at the International Council of Nurses Congress in 1912. The Foundation also organises the annual commemoration service held at WESTMINSTER ABBEY every May to celebrate nursing and midwifery.

## Rest of the UK

There are several statues to Florence in DERBY: outside the former Derby Royal Infirmary in LONDON ROAD, above the shops in ST PETER'S STREET and on the front of The Nightingale Home, a former maternity hospital, in TRINITY STREET. There is a stained-glass window in ST PETER'S CHURCH, a memorial plaque in DERBY CATHEDRAL, and a pavement star on the MADE IN DERBY TRAIL.

ROMSEY ABBEY in HAMPSHIRE has a stained-glass window, entitled *The Calling*, by the artist Sophie Hacker, which was unveiled in 2020 to commemorate the bicentenary of Florence's birth.

Florence had strong connections with LIVERPOOL and presented a bust of herself to the LIVERPOOL NURSING TRAINING SCHOOL in 1902. A stained-glass window featuring Florence and a District Nurse resides in the chapel of ROYAL LIVERPOOL HOSPITAL, having previously graced the old Royal Infirmary which closed in 1978. In 1913 a memorial to Florence commemorating her life and work was installed on PRINCES ROAD outside what was then the Central Home of the LIVERPOOL QUEEN VICTORIA DISTRICT NURSING ASSOCIATION.

A statue of Florence can be found in the GLASGOW ROYAL INFIRMARY in SCOTLAND and a blue plaque can be found on Malvernbury, on ABBEY ROAD in MALVERN, WORCESTERSHIRE, which

Florence visited to take the water treatments. Another plaque can be found in the spa town of HARROGATE, YORKSHIRE on YORK PLACE, where Florence also stayed to take the waters.

## Overseas

Florence despatched "Nightingale Nurses" to hospitals in AUSTRALIA, and the SYDNEY AND SYDNEY EYE HOSPITALS on Macquarie Street still has a Nightingale Wing. It also houses THE LUCY OSBURN-NIGHTINGALE MUSEUM which tells the history of nursing and medicine in Australia.

In 1975, a new hospital, known as the Florence Nightingale Hospital, was opened in KAISERSWERTH, GERMANY on the site where Florence had originally trained in 1851.

In honour of her birth place, a memorial to Florence was erected at the BASILICA DI SANTA CROCE in FLORENCE, ITALY in 1913.

The INTERNATIONAL COMMITTEE OF THE RED CROSS (ICRC), in GENEVA, SWITZERLAND instigated the FLORENCE NIGHTINGALE MEDAL in 1912. The world headquarters of the NIGHTINGALE INITIATIVE FOR GLOBAL HEALTH (NIGH) is also based in Switzerland, in LE GRAND-SACONNEX.

ISTANBUL in TURKEY has a FLORENCE NIGHTINGALE MUSEUM, which is housed in the barracks where Florence tended the sick and wounded in the Crimean War, and in HAIDAR PASHA CEMETERY a plaque was added to the CRIMEAN MEMORIAL in 1954 to celebrate the 100th anniversary of Florence's nursing work during the war.

Florence was consulted on and advised on the setting up of many nursing schools in the UNITED STATES OF AMERICA, including BELLEVUE HOSPITAL, NEW YORK, the CONNECTICUT TRAINING SCHOOL, NEW HAVEN and the BOSTON TRAINING SCHOOL at MASSACHUSETTS GENERAL HOSPITAL. She also corresponded with

John Shaw Billings to advise on his design of JOHNS HOPKINS UNIVERSITY HOSPITAL in BALTIMORE, MARYLAND, which opened in 1889. Florence was honoured in 1938 with a stained-glass window installed in the North Transept of the NATIONAL CATHEDRAL in WASHINGTON D.C., which features six scenes reflecting Florence's life and work.

---

**As the founder of modern nursing, Florence made nursing respectable. The most important legacy of Florence Nightingale is the many nurses worldwide, women and men, who have followed her into this valuable profession.**

# INDEX

## OF

# PEOPLE

## IN THE

## A TO Z

The index is intended to assist in finding people who are mentioned in the A to Z, particularly those mentioned at more than one location.

# PICTURE
# CREDITS

The majority of pictures have been reproduced by kind permission of the Florence Nightingale Museum: pages 9, 11, 19, 22, 28, 29, 30, 34, 41, 52, 54, 56, 59, 78, 82, 83, 84 and 94.

Grateful acknowledgement is also made to the following institutions and individuals:

Barts Health NHS Trust Archives and Museums: page 48.

Debbie Pearson: page 26.

Edward Stanford Ltd, London: page 37.

General Register Office: pages 27 and 58.

Julie Chandler: front cover, pages 26, 85 and 119, and back cover.

Look and Learn History Picture Archive, ©Look and Learn: pages 17 and 21.

National Portrait Gallery, London, ©National Portrait Gallery: page 39.

OpenStreetMap contributors at openstreetmap.org: pages 66, 68, 70, 72, 74

Public Domain: pages 37 and 47.

Royal Statistical Society, London: page 50.

The Headshot Guy: page 119.

Thomas Goode & Co., London: page 57.

Wellcome Collection, London, under CC BY 4.0: page 10.

Werner Houben, for his assistance with the maps: pages 66, 68, 70, 72, 74

Every effort has been made to contact all copyright holders. The publishers will be pleased to amend in future editions any errors or omissions brought to their attention.

# ACKNOWLEDGEMENTS

First of all, we would like to say a heartfelt Thank You to the Florence Nightingale Museum for their tremendous support with this book. We are especially grateful to David Green, Museum Director, and Hannah Smith, Museum Operations and Collections Coordinator, for generously sharing with us their time and expertise. They have lived the journey around *Florence Nightingale's London* with us, from the book's inception to its publication. Along the way, they have allowed us access to the Museum collection, provided suggestions and been incredibly enthusiastic of this project. We really could not have created this book without them – and all whilst working to save the Museum from permanent closure during the COVID-19 pandemic.

We would like to thank the world's leading expert on Florence Nightingale, Professor Lynn McDonald, of the University of Guelph, Ontario, Canada for the in-depth resources made available online – these have proved invaluable. The biography *Florence Nightingale: The Woman and Her Legend* by Mark Bostridge has also been a constant source of inspiration – for which, many thanks.

Other websites we have found extremely useful include: British History Online, Oxford Dictionary of National Biography, Lost Hospitals of London, Dr Orhan Aral's website on the Crimean War, and of course, the Florence Nightingale Museum.

We are also grateful to many individuals and organisations who have been generous with their advice, knowledge and support.

Peter Anderson read many a draft, helped with wordsmithing and was on the receiving end of numerous telephone calls. Joss Jowett and Lorrae McLeod, for venturing out onto the streets of London and checking the walk routes. Paul Blake, Rachel Kolsky, Robin Rowles, Tony Tucker and Margaret Willes for advice on publishing. Alex Price and Adam Waterton at the Royal Academy for information relating to Hilary Bonham Carter. William Hunt, Research Assistant to the Windsor Herald at the College of Arms for finally putting to rest the myth that Florence's father had been granted a coat of arms. Claire Jackson, Archivist at Thomas Goode & Co. for the guided tour and allowing us access to their ledgers. Kimberley Harsley, Archivist at NatWest Group Archives for information relating to Florence's bankers. Bryan Jones provided information about Florence's connections with Liverpool and also acted as photographic consultant. Clare Button, Dan Heather and Kate Jarman of Barts Health NHS Trust Archives and Museums for help relating to the German, London and Barts hospitals. Jude Brosnan at Stanfords for correspondence on irrigation maps of India. Taya Snow at Floris, for permission to use images of Florence's favourite perfume. Stian Westlake and Nicola Emmerson of the Royal Statistical Society for assistance with images of Florence's nomination for the Statistical Society of London.

As first-time authors, we cannot thank enough both designer Dominic Xavier and printers Blinky Media for being amazingly supportive throughout the design and publishing process.

And last but not least, we are very grateful for the encouragement of family and friends as we have brought this project to a conclusion.

# ABOUT
## THE
# AUTHORS

Debbie Pearson and Julie Chandler are experienced London tour guides. Julie worked with the Florence Nightingale Museum to devise their *Florence Nightingale's London* walking tour, which she has been leading with Debbie since 2019. During the pandemic, the walks were suspended, but Debbie and Julie's interest in Florence continued. When Debbie thought of writing this book, Julie was the obvious choice as co-author.

Debbie Pearson is a London tour guide who has been creating and leading guided walks and tours for many years. She qualified as a City of London Guide in 1999 and as a City of Westminster Guide in 2011. She also guides in the Guildhall Art Gallery. Debbie is an experienced lecturer, and has given illustrated talks on a variety of subjects, including wine, women and steamships. More recently she has ventured into the virtual realm, giving lectures online.

Julie Chandler is a London Blue Badge Tourist Guide and in 2010, founded London Town Tours, **www.londontowntours.london**. She is also a specialist City of London and City of Westminster Guide and a member of the Institute of Tourist Guiding and the British Guild of Tourist Guides. Julie regularly leads tours for visitors and Londoners in historic attractions and museums and on guided walks. She was delighted to feature in the BBC documentary *The Stuarts* delivering her walk on Charles I and the Civil War. Julie also gives lectures on a wide range of historical subjects and trains guides to deliver tours in a number of London visitor attractions.

If you would like a walking tour or talk (either in real-life or virtual), both Debbie and Julie can be contacted through the website **www.pearsonchandler.com**